the
wildlife-

Michael Chinery is a well-known naturalist and the author of numerous books on insects and garden wildlife, including *Collins Field Guide Insects of Britain and Northern Europe, Collins Nature Guide Garden Wildlife, Collins Complete British Insects* and *The Natural History of the Garden.* The latter was one of the first books to describe the whole range of wildlife to be found in the garden. Beyond the garden fence he is fascinated by all kinds of wildlife, and for several years he ran field courses designed to introduce people of all ages to the plant and animal life of the countryside.

the
wildlife-
friendly
garden

Michael Chinery

Collins

First published in 2004, this edition published in 2006 by Collins, an imprint of
HarperCollins*Publishers*
77–85 Fulham Palace Road
Hammersmith
London W6 8JB

The Collins website address is www.collins.co.uk

Collins is a registered trademark of HarperCollins Publishers Ltd.

09 08 07 06
9 8 7 6 5 4 3 2 1

A catalogue record of this book is available from the British Library.

ISBN-13 978 0 00 721597 3
ISBN-10 0 00 721597 5

This book was created by SP Creative Design for HarperCollins Publishers Ltd.
Editor: **Heather Thomas**
Design and production: **Rolando Ugolini**
Illustrations: **Acres Wild** pages 29, 30, 35 and **Rolando Ugolini** pages 81, 95, 118
Photography:
Acres Wild/Ian Smith: pages 28, 29, 31, 33, 34, 35t. **Ted Benton:** pages 103tr, 103br.
Michael Chinery: pages 6, 8, 9, 10, 11, 13, 14, 15, 16, 17b, 20b, 21, 22, 24, 25l, 26, 27t,
32, 35b, 36b, 37tr, 38, 39, 40, 41, 42, 43, 44, 47, 50l, 52b, 63t, 67, 68, 69, 71t, 84b, 85,
86, 87, 88, 89, 91b, 92, 93, 94, 95, 96, 97, 98, 99, 100, 101, 102, 103l, 114, 115, 116,
117, 118, 120, 121t, 122, 123l. **CJ Wildbird Foods/David White:** pages 12, 13, 36t, 45, 46r,
48, 49, 52t, 54, 55, 56r, 57, 58, 59, 61b, 62, 63b, 64, 65, 66, 70, 71b, 72, 73t, 73r, 74t, 75,
76, 77t, 77l, 78, 79, 80, 82, 83, 84t, 119, 123r. **Stan Dumican:** page 113bl. **Rolando
Ugolini:** pages 19, 20t, 25r, 27b, 68, 125. **Colin Varndell:** pages 13, 17t, 18, 37tl, 37b, 46l,
50r, 51, 53, 56l, 60, 61t, 73l, 74b, 77br, 90, 91t, 123t.
t=top, b=bottom, l=left, r=right
Front cover: Imagestate/Vanessa Cardui
Back cover: C J Wildbird Foods/David White
Colour reproduction by Colourscan, Singapore
Printed and bound by Lego, Italy

Contents

PART ONE

The Garden Habitat

All over the world, forests are being felled, wetlands are being drained, and heaths and grasslands are being ploughed up to make way for crops and houses. However, while these natural or semi-natural habitats are shrinking in the face of the increasing human population, one habitat – the garden – is increasing, and I think it is no exaggeration to say that today's gardens are our most important nature reserves.

Gardens cover almost a million hectares of the United Kingdom alone, and it is this enormous extent, as well as their great variety, that makes them such valuable wildlife refuges. In some areas, gardens are undoubtedly more important for wildlife than the surrounding 'countryside', with its pesticide-drenched monocultures. This is true even where the gardener does nothing in particular to encourage visitors: the wide range of plants cultivated in a typical garden is itself enough to attract lots of insects, and the insects bring in the birds.

Wildlife gardening aims to increase the number of native species visiting and residing in the garden, but it need not entail any loss of productivity. By being more laid-back and a little less tidy, you can have a garden buzzing with wildlife and filled with tasty crops and fine flowers. Your guests will actually do much of the pest control for you – free of charge!

Garden diversity

Although I have referred to the garden as a single habitat, on a par with a woodland or a meadow, most gardens are really very complex mixtures of habitats, each supporting its own rich assemblage of plant and animal life.

Flower beds

The flower border, a major feature of most gardens, contains a wide range of plants that flower at different times and attract insects and other small creatures for much of the year. Caterpillars chew the leaves, bugs suck the sap, bees and butterflies feast on the nectar, and many other insects attack the fruits and seeds. Hidden from view, the roots also provide sustenance for wireworms, leatherjackets, slugs, millipedes and numerous other creepy-crawlies, while earthworms derive most of their nourishment from the decaying plant matter in the soil. All of these small creatures provide food for

ABOVE: *Tiny mosses, seen here covered with pear-shaped spore capsules, erupt from the smallest cracks in walls and paths.*

birds and small mammals, so even a very simple flower border is really a mixture of several micro-habitats.

RIGHT: *Even the smallest of backyards can be a riot of colour, packed with flowers that act as filling stations for butterflies and many other insects.*

Vegetable plots

The vegetable plot has a similar diversity, although it does not have much in the way of nectar sources and, being subject to more disturbance as crops are planted and harvested, it tends to support a smaller variety of animal life in general.

Trees, shrubberies and hedges

These lend welcome shade and shelter to other parts of the garden and are micro-habitats in their own right, providing homes and hunting grounds for insects, spiders, birds and many other creatures.

Walls, fences and paths

These provide yet more living space for both flora and fauna, a fact that is easily appreciated when you look at the number of spider webs that adorn the fences in the autumn. Even concrete paths can support wildlife, tiny mosses wedge themselves into cracks in the concrete, while ants often nest underneath the paths and benefit from the heat absorbed by the concrete on sunny days – although you might not know that they are there until they fly off on their marriage flights in the summer.

> **CONSERVATION TIP**
>
> If you find a strange creature in your garden, don't assume it is harmful. Before squashing it with your foot, try to find out what it is and what it does. You will probably find that it is harmless or even useful – and then you won't need to squash it!

ABOVE: *Hit by the disappearance of so many farm and village ponds, many frogs find refuge in our garden ponds and mop up the slugs in return for the hospitality.*

Garden ponds

A pond is one of the richest of all wildlife habitats, and garden ponds are, happily, becoming increasingly popular. Pond-watching can be great fun, and the garden pond can literally be a life-saver for frogs, toads and dragonflies, all of which are now suffering from the disappearance of so many farm ponds and other watery sites in the countryside.

Go for variety

Not all of the visitors to your garden will be welcome guests, of course, but they will all add to the richness of the garden and the great majority will do no harm. They are just using your garden as a home. The more habitats you can create in your garden, the more guests you are likely to get, and the more diversity of wildlife. This can only be good for the wildlife population as a whole.

ABOVE: *A single climbing rose can feed a huge number of insects, which, in turn, can provide food for numerous spiders and birds. The birds may also nest there, well protected from predators by the rose's prickly stems.*

Wildlife-friendly gardens

Gardening for wildlife involves creating an approximation to one or more natural habitats that will be acceptable to birds and other wild creatures. It does not mean, however, giving the whole garden over to nature. You can continue to grow all your favourite flowers and vegetables in a wildlife garden.

Although a large garden can obviously support more plant and animal life than a small one, size is not that important. Even a small garden can contain several valuable wildlife habitats, such as a hedge, a small spinney or shrubbery, a pond and a grassy bank. It is what you plant in your garden that matters. Cultivated varieties and exotic plants certainly have a role in adding colour and excitement to a garden, but to be really wildlife friendly you do need to grow a selection of native shrubs and other plants. These are the species on which our native insects have evolved, and if you provide food for the insects, then you will indirectly feed many of our garden birds as well.

RIGHT: *The rough grass at the base of the wall in no way detracts from the appearance of this well-managed wildlife garden.*

Having created habitats for the insects and birds, you will need to minimize any disturbance. So be a little less enthusiastic with the lawn mower and the hedge trimmer. Does your lawn really need to look like a bowling green, and does it matter if the hedge is a bit rough around the edges? Don't be tempted to dead-head all of your plants; this might encourage a longer flowering season but it does deprive birds and insects of food and shelter. Bare soil needs weeding, so cover your garden with as much vegetation as you can; this will keep down the weeds and also give the birds a happy hunting ground. You might well find that wildlife-friendly gardening is gardener friendly as well!

ABOVE: *Let brambles scramble over your hedge. Insects will sip nectar from the flowers in summer and the birds, and you, will be able to enjoy the fruits later in the year.*

Keep wildlife safe

◆ **Household refuse** Be sure to pick up any bottles and cans left in the garden after a party, or just a well-earned drink. Apart from the risk of causing injury to yourself or your family, these containers can become coffins for small animals.

ABOVE: *The great green bush-cricket is a noisy inhabitant of the many undisturbed garden hedges and shrubberies that exist both on the European continent and in southern England.*

Thousands of shrews and other small mammals die every year in carelessly abandoned bottles. Getting in to sample the dregs is easy, but climbing the smooth sides to get out again certainly is not. Drink cans are not quite so bad, but beetles and many other useful creatures regularly drown in them.

◆ **Fruit bushes and netting** If you need to put nets over your fruit bushes, do make sure that they are taut and well anchored so that birds and other animals cannot get tangled up in them.

◆ **Weedkillers and pesticides** If you cannot survive without using weedkillers or other pesticides, be sure to follow the instructions carefully, and to dispose of any dregs where they cannot do any harm. It is very easy to kill vegetation and its associated animal life by careless application of pesticides, especially in windy conditions when sprays can drift far from their intended targets.

CONSERVATION TIP

Don't use peat in your garden. Our peat bogs have shrunk alarmingly over the last 100 years or so because of the demand for peat, and their wildlife has dwindled accordingly. Plenty of alternatives to peat are on the market now, and for hanging baskets there is 'Supermoss' – a sphagnum substitute made from recycled cloth and paper pulp.

A healthy garden

It took millions of years for nature to build up an equilibrium, in which each plant and animal species has its place and in which each helps to keep the rest under control. Nothing lives alone in nature, for every creature either eats or is eaten by one or more other creatures. We have destroyed much of this delicate balance, but it is still not too late to put the process into reverse.

Restoring the balance

The key thing is to live and work with nature, steering it in the direction we want in our gardens instead of destroying it completely. If we can achieve an approximation to nature's balance of predators and prey, then no one species will be able to multiply to such an extent that it becomes a nuisance. By creating some natural habitats in your garden you will inevitably attract their characteristic wildlife. Trees and shrubs, for example,

WHAT GOOD ARE MOSQUITOES?

This question is commonly asked by many people who have been bitten by these insects. Mosquitoes don't do us any good, of course, but, in common with all other living things, they form part of nature's intricate web and have a role to play in nature's economy. From the point of view of a hungry swallow or a stickleback, mosquitoes are actually quite good!

attract birds; ponds are magnets for frogs and toads; and flower beds pull in many colourful insects. These guests will add considerable interest to your garden and will also do much to keep down the less desirable visitors – the pests. They will not eradicate the pests, but the amount of damage is likely to be minimal and you will be able to boast a healthy garden with a balanced ecology.

RIGHT: *Although few of these young spiders, just hatched from their eggs, will survive to become adults, undoubtedly they will eat a lot of insects before themselves falling prey to various enemies.*

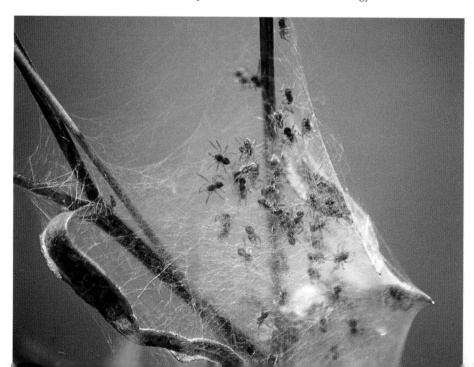

A TYPICAL GARDEN FOOD WEB

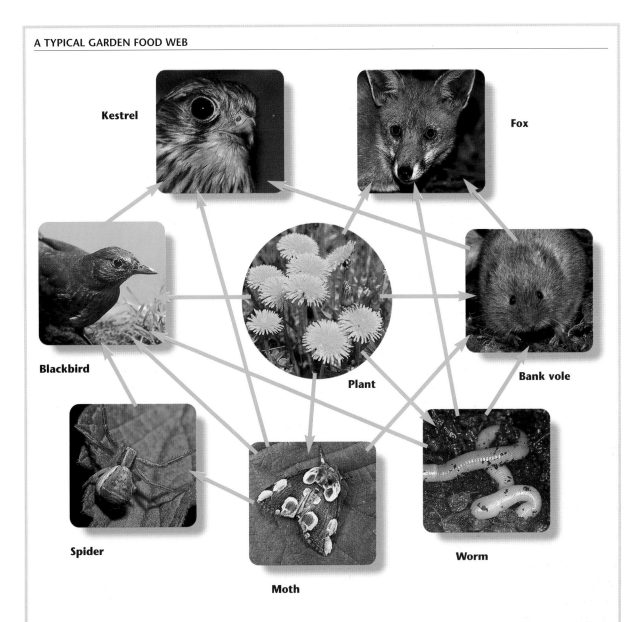

Kestrel

Fox

Blackbird

Plant

Bank vole

Spider

Moth

Worm

ABOVE: Moth feeds on nectar; spider eats moth; blackbird eats spider. This is a typical food chain. Another example might be plant; insect; vole; fox. Many more such chains can be observed in the garden, and it quickly becomes obvious that these chains are all linked together in a web – because most animals eat more than one kind of food. Blackbirds, for example, are equally happy with earthworms and elderberries, while the bank vole may vary its normally vegetarian diet with snails and fungi as well as insects. Just a few of the chains in a garden food web are illustrated here, with the arrows pointing from the food to the consumers. You will find that each chain starts with a plant. With each species kept in check by its predators and/or food supplies, the whole community remains in a healthy equilibrium.

Garden friends and foes

Older nature books commonly listed the gardener's friends and foes, but now that we know a lot more about the life histories of the animals and know that everything has its place in nature's complex web, it is not so easy to pigeon-hole them in this way. For example, a centipede eating a harmful slug might be regarded as a friend, but you might change your opinion on discovering that a centipede's diet consists mainly of other centipedes. Nevertheless, it is still possible to recognize some positively useful creatures – friends – which should be welcomed into the garden and some without which our gardens would be better off. These are the pests that eat our crops and spread diseases and they must be discouraged if not actually destroyed.

Our friends

◆ **Ground beetles** These long-legged, fast-moving insects are most likely to be found lurking under logs and stones. They hunt by night, destroying slugs and many harmful caterpillars.
◆ **Lacewings** In spite of their fragile appearance, the lacewings are voracious carnivores, destroying hundreds or even thousands of greenfly during their lives.
◆ **Hedgehogs** Among our most popular garden inhabitants, hedgehogs do good service by getting rid of slugs and snails, although they do destroy the useful earthworms as well.
◆ **Ladybirds** These attractive little beetles eat huge numbers of greenfly and other

BELOW: *Lacewings often come to lighted windows at night; introduce them to your roses or other plants where they can eat the troublesome aphids.*

ABOVE: *A good friend in the garden, this hedgehog is busily polishing off a snail.*

RIGHT: *Long, sensitive antennae enable the ground beetle to track down its prey at night.*

harmful aphids and are therefore among the gardener's best friends.

◆ **Centipedes** These fast-moving carnivores eat a wide range of other creatures, including slugs, insect grubs and other centipedes, which they kill with powerful venom. On balance, they do more good than harm, and they are certainly not dangerous to us.

Our foes

◆ **Lily beetles** These colourful beetles destroy the leaves and seed capsules of all kinds of lilies. What look like slimy black droppings on the plants are actually the lily beetle grubs which are covered with their own excrement.

◆ **Aphids** These tiny bugs occur in huge numbers and they deform many plants by sucking out the sap. They also spread numerous viruses responsible for diseases such as potato leaf roll and various mosaics. There are hundreds of species.

◆ **Leatherjackets** These rather featureless grey creatures are the grubs of crane-flies or daddy-long-legs. They live in the soil, especially under lawns and flower beds, and destroy the roots.

◆ **Cabbage white caterpillars** The black and yellow caterpillars are the larvae of the large white butterfly. Living in large clusters, they can quickly reduce a cabbage leaf to just a skeleton, and they contaminate the rest of the plant with an unpleasant smell.

◆ **Slugs** Perhaps the most hated of all our garden residents, the slugs nibble their way through our flowers and vegetables with equal enthusiasm. But not all slugs are pests: some of them prefer rotting leaves and fungi (see page 43).

LEFT: *Beautiful, but also beastly, the lily beetle must go if you value your lilies.*

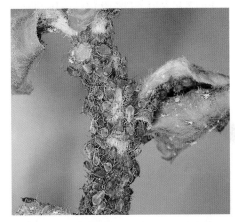

LEFT: *This apple shoot has been deformed by the piercing beaks of hundreds of sap-sucking aphids.*

LEFT: *Caterpillars of the large white butterfly here surround a solitary caterpillar of the small white. Both species are major pests of cabbages and other brassicas.*

LEFT: *One of the worst of the gardener's foes: the netted slug is the one we usually find in our lettuces.*

Pest control

Gardening will always be a competition, with the gardener pitting his or her wits against an assortment of uninvited guests which are doing their best to damage the plants. Although you may have to get tough from time to time, it need not be all-out war. Live and let live is always a good motto for the gardener.

Avoid chemicals

One can buy chemicals, i.e. poison, to control just about every garden visitor, but they have many drawbacks. There is always a risk of killing useful or harmless creatures as well as pests. Killing useful creatures, such as ladybirds, may actually lead to an increase in the garden's aphid population and a tendency to use ever increasing doses of insecticide. Although most modern pesticides break down rapidly in the soil, heavy applications

may lead to a build-up of residues that can damage the soil and enter the food chains, where they can have far-reaching and surprising effects. Killing harmless creatures does have a knock-on effect by denying birds and other animals their natural food, so your garden will be much less interesting. The true wildlife gardener uses non-poisonous means to discourage or get rid of pests. Aphids, for example, can usually be controlled simply by squashing them with your fingers.

Cultural control

Adjusting the way you grow things, or even what you grow, can make your garden less attractive to pests. Most weeds, for example, can be eliminated by spreading a layer of chipped bark or compost over the garden. You can try growing red cabbage instead of the traditional green varieties: this may not

RIGHT: *Re-cycling the empties: this lacewing larva, pictured with its jaws plunged into an aphid, camouflages itself by piling the empty skins of its victims on its back.*

BIOLOGICAL CONTROL

Biological control, which uses natural enemies to keep pests in check, can be wonderfully effective. Introducing ladybirds and their larvae to your garden, for example, can wipe out an infestation of aphids in days. A single ladybird larva may eat 500 aphids in its three-week development. Green lacewings (see page 126 for stockists) do a good job on summer populations of aphids, and are useful in greenhouses throughout the year.

Biological control of slugs, which are surely at the top of most gardeners' hit-lists, can now be achieved simply by

ABOVE: *Song thrush*

using a minute parasitic worm called *Plasmarhabditis hermaphrodita*. Available through good garden centres and other suppliers (see page 126), the worms seek out slugs and bore their way in. They multiply rapidly and the slugs literally explode, releasing another generation of worms to carry on the work. It is unlikely that the worms will move out into surrounding areas in the numbers required for slug control, so the hedgehog population will not go hungry.

Snails can be kept in check by song thrushes as long as you have sufficient anvils on which the birds can break the shells. If you have no concrete paths or rockery stones, lay a few bricks or large stones around the garden and listen for the tapping as the birds get to work.

deter the cabbage white caterpillars, but at least you can see them more easily and remove them before they do the damage!

Companion planting or inter-planting is often used to reduce damage by pests. Planting onions and carrots close together works well because the smell of the carrots deters or confuses the damaging onion-fly, and the smell of the onions discourages the carrot-fly. Roses or other flowers planted at the ends of vegetable rows attract hover-flies, which may lay eggs on aphid-infested crops. Some hover-fly larvae can demolish the aphids at a rate of one every minute!

Doing nothing and allowing nature's web to keep the pests in check is probably the best method of all. Surely losing a few

plants to beetles and caterpillars is a price well worth paying for a garden which is teeming with wildlife and with no risk of poisoning yourself or your family?

BELOW: *Roses are often planted in vineyards. Hover-flies, which are attracted to the flowers, lay their eggs on the surrounding vines, where their grubs attack harmful aphids and other pests.*

Planning your garden

An abandoned garden soon becomes clothed with nettles, brambles and other invasive plants. Birds and some other animals may appreciate such a wilderness, but your neighbours certainly will not. Diversity is also lost. Good wildlife gardens are planned, not abandoned.

BELOW: *A planned garden does not have to be very formal. The position of this garden pond was actually carefully planned, but the plantlife gives it a wonderfully wild and natural appearance.*

A wilderness and a wildlife garden are not the same! A wilderness, often defined as a wild and confused mass of vegetation, certainly does not exhibit the variety at the heart of a wildlife garden. It may have advantages for some animals, including the hedgehog and various birds, and there may be short-term advantages for some insects but, if left untouched, the wilderness will succumb to the processes of natural succession and will turn into woodland in 20 years or so. If you want a garden wilderness, restrict it to a particular area and be prepared to tame it occasionally. And plan the rest of your wildlife garden carefully to make the best use of the available space.

The wildlife garden cannot be ideal for everything; it has to be a compromise. However, by growing lots of different plants you can create wonderful wildlife homes and still have some room for your favourite flowers and vegetables. And you can do this even in a small garden.

Plan it on paper

Decide what features you want to include, which, in practice, usually means what you have room for, and then measure your garden carefully so that you can draw an accurate scale plan. Your aim should be to have the flower beds and other more formal or tidier parts of your garden near to the house and let them grade into the wilder-looking areas further away. This will give the whole garden a natural look and still allow you to control its structure. Remember that the pond should be in an open spot and that bird tables should be positioned where you can watch them in comfort.

When you have decided where everything is to go, you can start thinking about the plants. The soil will influence what you can grow, so have a look at neighbouring gardens and the surrounding countryside to determine which plants do well in the area. You can also use the Internet to find out which members of your local flora are worth planting in your garden (see page 127). Although native species are best (see page 10), you don't have to ignore exotic species altogether. They lend superb colour to the garden and can provide just as much shelter for wildlife as our native species. Many also provide seasonal nectar and fruit.

Trees and hedges

Woodland margins are among the richest of all wild habitats, and an excellent way to reproduce them in your garden is to plant a hedge with a wavy margin, preferably on either the northern or the eastern boundary, or both, as this will help provide protection from cold winds without casting too much shade. It will also enable you to grow primroses, foxgloves and many other sun-loving flowers at the base. Include as many different shrubs in your hedge as you can, as this will increase its attractiveness to both birds and insects (see page 24). A 'mini-spinney', with three or four small trees, is another excellent way to mimic the woodland edge.

Ideally, the hedge should be on your northern boundary, but remember your neighbours: shelter for you might mean shade for them. Birch is a good tree in such a situation because it does not cast deep shade. It also supports over 200 insect species in Britain, and several small birds enjoy its seeds in the autumn. Alder and hawthorn are nearly as effective in

BELOW: *Among the most beautiful of all our spring flowers, the primrose graces the bottoms of many garden hedgerows. Look out for the furry bee-fly plumbing the flowers for nectar with its long, rigid tongue.*

RIGHT: Just a few small trees on the edge of the garden can provide food and shelter for many creatures normally found in a woodland habitat, especially if the herbage is left uncut until autumn.

RIGHT: Bird cherry is an excellent tree for the wild garden. It can reach a height of 15 m (45 ft), but it does not cast a dense shade and it is easily kept in check by regular trimming. Laden with heavily-scented flowers in spring, the bird cherry bears shiny black fruits later in the year.

this respect. Rowan, bird cherry, hazel and crab apple are other good trees for this situation, or you could try planting a cultivated apple; even a good cooker can support plenty of wildlife, from tiny insects to collared doves, and you can also enjoy the fruit yourself.

Garden paths

These can be made of brick or concrete, or paving slabs laid as stepping stones across the lawn or through the flower beds. For a more natural look, however, you can use chipped bark laid over a firmly-rolled base and retained by a kerb of rustic poles. You can disguise the edge

LEFT: *Bugle makes a colourful edging to a garden path in the spring. The wild form and the various cultivars are equally attractive to bees.*

a little by planting violets and bugle here and there and allowing them to tumble over the poles. Some interesting fungi may well spring up on the poles and on the chippings.

Try to make the paths curve through the garden so that you get new views at every turn and possibly a feeling that you are in a larger area. However, if you cannot do this, you can create an illusion of distance on a straight path by using large chips near the house and smaller ones further away. If your path is on a slope, put in some wooden steps here and there. Old railway sleepers are ideal, and if you drill a few holes in them you will probably attract various solitary bees (see page 118). You can also drill holes for them in the path edging.

Pergolas

Although pergolas tend to be associated mainly with formal gardens, they can actually be wonderful wildlife centres. Clothed with roses or honeysuckle in summer, they attract lots of insects and insect-eating birds, and some birds will

readily nest in the dense climbers. You can make pergolas work for you in the winter as well by hanging an assortment of bird feeders on them. The sturdy uprights also make good supports for nest-boxes, but it is as well to move the feeders to another site before the nesting season begins: hordes of birds squabbling over a nearby bag of peanuts are not likely to make your nest-boxes desirable residences. Solitary bees and wasps will also appreciate your pergola if you drill a few small holes in the woodwork.

BELOW: *Pergolas allowed to become overgrown with an assortment of creepers can be superb for garden birds.*

A wildlife meadow

In the middle of the twentieth century, flower-rich meadows could be found in many parts of Britain, but less than two per cent of the meadows that delighted us in the 1940s survive today. Unfortunately, we cannot put them back, but every little helps and a flowery lawn in your garden is a good start.

Put your mower away for a few weeks and you will certainly get some new flowers on your lawn, but unless your garden is on a chalk or limestone slope you probably will not grow much more than dandelions and daisies initially. To create a good flower-rich habitat you will have to introduce most of the flowers.

Scattering seeds into an existing lawn is not likely to achieve very much because the grasses will swamp the young seedlings, although you can increase their chances by removing the turf from small areas before sowing. Therefore a better way is to stick established plants into your lawn, but even then they are likely to be overshadowed. The best approach of all is to strip all the turf and much of the top-soil away and then re-seed the ground with a mixture of grass and flower seeds. Make sure that the grass mixture does not include rye grass, which is too vigorous for a wildflower meadow.

Do not be tempted to sow too many species in a new lawn: four or five grasses and half a dozen flower species are plenty. Spread the grass seeds evenly over the area, but for a natural appearance the flower seeds should be sown in drifts of just two or three species. Never add any fertilizer to your meadow – this will merely encourage the grasses to grow and overshadow the other plants.

Choose your species

The chart opposite lists some of the most useful and attractive flowers for your meadow, but what you can grow successfully obviously depends on the soil. One sure way to find out what might be best for you is to have a good look at the surrounding countryside, including the roadside verges. Flowers that grow well there are likely to do well in your meadow. You can collect the seeds by shaking the ripe seed-heads into paper bags, but never dig up the wild plants. If you have access to the Internet you can

BELOW: *Abandon your mower and you will soon acquire a grassland jungle similar to this, where field mouse-ear and bird's-foot trefoil are flowering below the thistles and tall flower-heads of the grasses.*

call up a website that allows you to see a list of all the plants growing in your area just by inserting the first half of your postcode (see page 127). It also tells you whether the plants are garden-worthy and lists the suppliers of native plant seeds. It is very important always to use native seeds; foreign seeds, even if they are of the same species, may be adapted to different conditions and their genes may contaminate and damage our native flora.

Sow your seeds in the autumn, but do not expect a mass of colour in the first summer – many seeds will not even germinate until the spring, and the young plants need a full season's growth before they are ready to flower.

Management is vital

Meadows were originally created by grazing and/or cutting, so you need to cut your flower meadow at least once a year. Use a scythe or a strimmer if possible, but if you have to use a mower make sure that the blades are not set too low.

◆ Cut in late summer or autumn for a good display of spring flowers, such as cuckoo flower, cowslip, fritillary, bugle and dandelion.

◆ Cut in spring and autumn for summer colour from the likes of knapweed, lady's bedstraw, scabious, meadow cranesbill and ox-eye daisy.

Always leave the cut vegetation on the ground for a day or two to allow any seeds to fall, but then make sure you clear it all away because a good flower meadow depends on poor soil fertility.

If you are lucky enough to have a large meadow area, you can mow paths

through it more frequently so that you can enjoy the flowers at close quarters.

An area of long grass can look untidy even if it is full of flowers, so it is a good plan to mow the edge to stop the grass from tumbling on to your path or drive. You might like to mow the area nearest to the house as well and allow it to merge gradually into the longer grass, much as a golf course fairway grades into the rough.

If you live in open countryside, you could even construct a ha-ha boundary (a sunken fence or ditch) so that your wild meadow appears to drift off into the surrounding fields.

ABOVE: *Drifts of delicate pink cuckoo flowers adorn many areas of damp grassland in the spring, and they are often accompanied by bright yellow cowslips.*

ABOVE: *The meadow cranesbill is one of the most beautiful of our grassland species. It does best on lime-rich soils, where its bright violet-blue flowers can be seen throughout the summer.*

MEADOW PLANTS

These native plants are suitable for you to plant in your wildlife meadow:

- Bladder campion
- Cuckoo flower*
- Greater knapweed
- Meadow cranesbill
- Self heal
- Cowslip
- Field scabious
- Ox-eye daisy
- Ragged robin*
- Yarrow

Plants marked * will thrive in damp areas.

The garden hedge

Most houses come complete with some sort of boundary feature – a hedge or a wall if you are lucky, but more often a relatively barren wooden fence. Although walls and fences can support a limited range of plant and animal life, a mature hedgerow is a thriving community, teeming with insects and other animals. At the same time it can give you privacy and protect your garden from the wind.

You could consider enriching your garden by replacing your fence with a hedge, but only if the neighbours agree! Alternatively, you could plant a low hedge inside your boundary or instal one as the garden equivalent of a room-divider – separating your vegetables from your flower beds perhaps. Hedges are very cheap to create, although they do need more maintenance than walls and fences.

ABOVE: *The nests of caterpillars of the small eggar moth were once common on roadside hawthorn hedges, but mechanical trimming in summer has caused the species to become rare. Garden hedges may be its salvation.*

ABOVE: *Although it is very conspicuous when viewed on a bare twig, the 10 cm (4 in) caterpillar of the privet hawkmoth is surprisingly hard to spot in a privet hedge.*

What to plant

Although exotic species may bear plenty of tasty berries for the birds, they do not support many insects (see page 10), so native shrubs are best. Hawthorn is good as it grows quickly, even from cuttings, and it is eaten by more than 150 insect species in Britain alone. Blackthorn, field maple, spindle, dogwood, buckthorn, alder buckthorn and guelder rose are also good. You can encourage honeysuckle, brambles and wild roses to scramble over the hedge. In fact, the more species you can incorporate, the better.

The animal residents

A hedge is both a home and larder for numerous garden animals.

◆ **Birds** Song thrushes, blackbirds, greenfinches, dunnocks and long-tailed tits all nest in garden hedges. The last two are happy to nest among slender twigs, but the others like to build in a stout fork and are most likely to nest in older hedges. Many more birds find food among the branches.

◆ **Mammals** Hedgehogs, shrews, mice and voles all forage in the leaf litter at the base of the hedge. Stoats and weasels – Europe's smallest carnivores – may also hunt there.

LEFT: *The cultivated* Prunus *shrubs which make up this superb garden hedge are just as good for nesting birds as the wild shrubs.*

◆ **Insects** These abound in the hedgerow and they play a vital role in feeding the local bird population. However, you will need a keen eye to spot the twig-like caterpillars of the geometrid moths, such as the swallowtailed moth and some of the thorn moths. The hairy and colourful caterpillars of the vapourer, grey dagger and yellowtail moths are much easier to find. Most birds will avoid these hairy caterpillars because the hairs of some species can cause severe irritation. Spiders thrive on the insect life, although we tend not to notice these fascinating small garden creatures until the autumn when their webs are more visible (see page 123).

GARDEN PROJECT – PLANTING A HEDGE FOR WILDLIFE

A hedge is best planted in the winter, and all the plants should be pruned to no more than about 30 cm (12 in) in height after planting them to encourage the growth of interlocking shoots. Don't be too eager with your secateurs after that. A hedge does need to be trimmed from time to time, but if you want a really good wildlife hedge then you should do this only once every two years.

By doing this, you will always have some one-year-old wood on which many of the shrubs carry their flowers. It is a good plan to trim half the hedge one winter and the other half the next. Try to keep your hedge narrower at the top than at the bottom; otherwise the ground flora may become shaded out and some of the lower branches may die back and leave gaps.

Wildlife walls

Although, as a home for wildlife, a hedge beats a wall every time, there is still a place for a wall in a wildlife garden. This is particularly true on sloping ground, where small walls, no more than a metre (three feet) or so high, can be used to create a very attractive terraced effect.

You don't need to be an expert bricklayer; in fact, you don't really need bricks at all. You can try building a dry stone wall, using one of the many traditional styles that are found in upland Britain. Always use local stone if possible, as this fits into the landscape so much better than alien material. You may be able to buy large stones from a local quarry or a nearby garden centre. Failing this, get hold of *The Natural Stone Directory* (see page 127) which will tell you where you can buy almost every kind of stone.

A wildlife refuge

Because there is no mortar between the stones, except perhaps at the ends of the wall, the dry stone wall offers homes to a huge variety of animals: lizards bask and hunt on the wall by day, while toads hide in the cool recesses along with numerous spiders and beetles.

Bumblebees will also take up residence, and in the warmer parts of Europe they may be joined by the harmless little scorpion *Euscorpius flavicaudis*.

LEFT: *This section of a dry stone wall shows the large through stones which are used to tie the two faces of the wall together. The central cavity can be filled with soil or small stones.*

BELOW: *Red valerian is an attractive, although rather invasive, inhabitant of old walls. It attracts lots of butterflies and moths.*

ABOVE: *The scorpion* Euscorpius flavicaudis *inhabits old walls in southern Europe. You may see the pincers sticking out of a crevice.*

LEFT: *The black redstart, uncommon in Britain but a common garden bird on the continent of Europe, regularly breeds in holes and crevices in old walls. Its nest is an untidy and none-too-secure pile of grass, which is lined with hair and feathers.*

Wrens, black redstarts, great tits and pied wagtails are among the many birds that may find your wall to their liking.

The hedgehog is sure to find a snug retreat among the lower stones. And don't forget yourself either: it is not difficult to incorporate a smooth stone slab in the wall so that you can sit comfortably and watch your garden guests.

Water your wall with a slurry of cow or horse dung after building it to encourage invasion by mosses and lichens, which then act as nurseries for ferns and other plants. It will soon become a home for wildlife.

GARDEN PROJECT – BUILDING A DRY STONE WALL

If your garden is flat, you can use low stone walls simply as decorative features or to create raised beds. Such beds are ideal for alpines and many other plants and, once built, they make gardening much easier as well! Old bricks can be used instead of stone, but you still do not need mortar. Dig out the wall base to a depth of one brick, making sure that it is fairly level and compacted down.

To retain a bed, the wall should be double thickness and no higher than four courses. Set each course of bricks on a mixture of sand and peat-free compost. Leave a few gaps between the bricks for lizards and other small creatures to get in, but otherwise the bricks in each course need to be in contact with each other.

You will not have to wait long for ferns and other plants to spring up naturally in the sand/compost mixture and bind the bricks firmly together, but you can speed things up by planting some yourself. You'll find that houseleeks and stonecrops do very well on these walls. Remember that this wall is not for walking or climbing on!

ABOVE: *This very simple low wall is made of old bricks which are laid double thickness and across each other to bind and strengthen the wall. Leave some small gaps in between.*

The garden pond

If you have room to create only one semi-natural habitat in your garden, then I think it should be a garden pond. This is one of the richest of all habitats in terms of wildlife. As well as providing homes for frogs, newts, dragonflies and many other exciting creatures, it provides food, drink and bathing facilities for birds and assorted mammals. And all will give you, the gardener, a great deal of fun.

BELOW: *Surrounded by a rich variety of wild and cultivated marginal plants, including yellow irises and brilliant orange primulas, this pond will attract a wide range of insects and other wildlife, and there is enough open water to encourage frogs and dragonflies to come and lay their eggs.*

If you are really lucky your garden might already have a stream that you can dam to make a small pond. Local rocks can be used to form the dam, or you can utilize a tree trunk. Oak and elm are good for this as both timbers survive well under water. A height of about 50 cm (20 in) is fine for the dam. Be sure to consult the appropriate authorities if you want to create a larger pool because anything more than a small dam could interfere with water supplies further downstream.

Most of us have to create our ponds from scratch, but this is not difficult if there are strong people to do the digging. Pond plants and animals like plenty of sunshine, so don't site your pond under trees. Apart from creating a lot of shade, they will drop their leaves into the water in the autumn and cause a lot of problems. If you compare a woodland pool with one in the open, you will be in no doubt that the latter is a much richer and more attractive habitat.

Constructing the pond

Ponds dug in low-lying areas where the water table is close to the surface sometimes fill themselves, and you can't ask for much more natural ponds than these. Otherwise you will have to line your pond.

Preformed fibreglass liner

If you decide on a preformed fibreglass liner, all you have to do is to buy one of the shape and size that you want, dig a similarly-shaped hole, and drop the liner into it (see below). A morning's work can give you a very attractive pond!

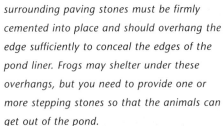

RIGHT: *This cross-section of a pre-formed fibreglass pond shows the correct level for a shelf for marginal plants. The surrounding paving stones must be firmly cemented into place and should overhang the edge sufficiently to conceal the edges of the pond liner. Frogs may shelter under these overhangs, but you need to provide one or more stepping stones so that the animals can get out of the pond.*

1 Mark the position of the pond with pegs and string or a line of sand for irregular shapes.

2 The excavation must match the profile of the unit. Measure all depths carefully from the rim.

3 Allow for installation of the pool and back-filling by digging out a larger hole than marked.

4 After removing all stones, make sure that the ground is compacted down.

5 Smooth the sides and spread a 5 cm (2 in) protective layer of sand on the base and sides.

6 Press the unit gently until level, then part-fill with water and back-fill with sifted soil or sand.

Flexible liners

These liners allow you to have a pond of virtually any shape you like. You can use heavy-duty black polythene, but butyl rubber is a better material and, although considerably more expensive, it is likely to last much longer. Whatever you get, make sure it has at least a ten-year guarantee.

Calculating the liner size

You can calculate the required liner size by measuring the maximum length and breadth of the pond, adding twice the maximum depth to each dimension, and then adding a further 50 cm (20 in) to each to allow for sufficient overlap at the pond's margins. Although you can choose whatever shape you like, butyl rubber liners are usually rectangular, so long, narrow ponds tend to be rather wasteful of this lining material.

WHICH WATER SOURCE?

The tap is usually the only source of water for the pond. The high mineral content of tap water may encourage the algae to multiply rapidly and turn the water green in the summer, but this will not harm the wildlife of the pond and the algae will gradually dwindle as they use up the minerals. The best thing, if you are planning to have a pond, is to store up a supply of rain water ready for filling it. Always use rain water to top up your pond in the summer: an adaptor fitted to a drainpipe can be used to divert water into a hose leading to the pond.

Moisture-loving shrubs, such as guelder rose and alder buckthorn, can be planted around the pond, but do not let them shade the water

Free-floating plants, such as frogbit, provide shade for many small animals

The floating leaves of yellow water lily and similar plants make good landing pads for dragonflies

Large stones breaking the surface provide perches for drinking birds and basking spots for frogs

A sloping 'beach' makes it easy for animals to get in and out of the pond

Native marginal plants, such as arrowhead and flowering rush, can be planted in the swampy area at the edge. They give a natural effect and provide cover for many animals

The jetty can be supported on building blocks, but these should be set on rubber or plastic pads to protect the liner

Submerged plants, such as curled pondweed and water milfoil, maintain oxygen levels

The flexible liner can be covered with fine soil here and there to allow plants to root naturally

Wetland plants, such as marsh marigold, provide food and shelter for insects and many other small creatures

1 Decide on the shape and size of your pond and mark it out with a rope or a hose-pipe before you begin digging. Make the pond as big as you can, but ensure that you can get a liner of a suitable size before you start work!

2 Make sure that the edges of the pond are perfectly level, otherwise the liner will be exposed in some places. The central area should be at least 50 cm (20 in) deep to ensure that the whole pond does not freeze solid in a hard winter.

3 It is best to start digging in the centre and then slope the bottom gently up to the surface. Leave a flat shelf about 15 cm (6 in) below the final water surface on one side, so you can grow marginal plants there in pots (see page 29).

PROTECT YOUR LINER

Before installing the liner, remove any sharp stones that you can see and then line the hole with soft sand to protect the liner. You can also buy polyester matting specifically made for this purpose. Alternatively, you can use old plastic bags, as used for potting compost, but an old carpet is even better.

4 It's now time to install the liner by spreading it over the hole and pushing it roughly into position. Weight the edges down with something heavy, ensuring that there is at least 25 cm (10 in) overlap all round the margin. Then you can start adding the water. As it runs in, the weight of the water stretches the liner and moulds it to the shape of the hole.

5 When the pond is full, you can tidy up the margins, concealing the edges of the liner under concrete, stone slabs, turf, or large pebbles. If you use slabs, make sure that at least some are low enough for animals to escape from the pond. Slabs should also slope away from the water, so that the rain cannot wash soil and other debris into the pond.

6 Leave everything to settle for a few days after filling the pond. If any of the lining is still visible, cover it up. Exposed lining looks unattractive and, more importantly, exposure to strong sunlight can damage a polythene liner. When you are satisfied that the margins are all level and they are properly covered, you can start planting your pond.

RIGHT: *This moorhen's nest has been built on a small rocky island in the middle of a pond. The bird is about to sit on the eggs, which the other parent has just left.*

Creating an island

If you are planning a large pond, you might like to create an island on which moorhens can nest. The easiest way to do this is to leave a mound of soil in the middle, with a flat top just below the eventual water surface. The liner will go right over it, so remember to add twice the height of the mound to each dimension of the liner! Put a cluster of logs or smooth stones and some potted water plants on top of the liner to finish off the island.

In smaller ponds I have found that a log of oak or elm, cut to such a length that it can be wedged across the pond, makes an excellent 'island'. It provides an 'escape hatch' for frogs and for animals that might fall in, and also provides a nice drinking spot for birds. Dragonflies may perch on it and some may even lay eggs while there.

CLEANING AND MAINTAINING YOUR POND

Well-sited ponds with a good balance of plants and animals should not need much maintenance, but most garden ponds do need attention from time to time. Excess vegetation should be removed in the autumn. Rotting leaves use up oxygen, causing the bottom of the pond to become black and smelly, so make sure that dead vegetation is removed in the autumn before the frogs start to settle down in the mud for the winter. Leave the material on the side for a day or two so that any animals in it can find their way back to the water.

Green algae often turn pond water green in the summer. This is not harmful, but it does make pond-watching difficult. The problem is most common in ponds without a good growth of submerged plants to use up the nutrients. Several ecologically friendly products are available to combat the problem, but first try adding a bundle of barley straw to your pond. As the straw breaks down, it releases substances that appear to kill the algae. You can get the straw at good aquatic centres, together with information on the quantities needed.

Creating a marsh garden

Many natural ponds are surrounded by marshy areas, and it is quite easy to create this habitat around your garden pond when you are constructing it.

If you are using a flexible liner, dig a shallow extension, 20–25 cm (8–10 in) deep, at one end or side of the pond, leaving a ridge between the two excavations. This ridge should be a few centimetres below the final water level, and the liner should be spread over it and into the shallow marsh area.

Edge the latter with turf or stone to the same level as the edge of the pond, and then create a barrier between the pond and the extension with a large oak or elm log laid on the ridge or a couple of courses of bricks (without mortar) topped by turf or stone slabs.

Mix the excavated soil with some good compost, ensuring that it is free from sharp stones, and then return it to the incipient marsh. Fill the pond with water (see page 31). It will seep into the marsh, but the barrier should stop the soil running into the pond. Do not create a marsh all round your pond; you need a certain amount of firm ground on which to stand or sit and watch the pondlife.

You can make an independent marsh garden by putting a liner into a hole and filling it with soil. The hole should be about 50 cm (20 in) deep to it retain sufficient moisture in dry weather, although you can top it up with a hose if necessary.

Mud-loving plants

Marsh marigolds, purple loosestrife, yellow iris, bogbean, ragged robin and water mint will all grow happily in the waterlogged soil of your marsh and will attract lots of insects. Frogs and toads enjoy the food and shelter in this watery habitat, and they will control the slugs in other parts of your garden.

LEFT: *A mixture of wild and cultivated flowers can produce a riot of colour in a marsh garden.*

Stocking your pond

A natural pond will normally have three ecological groups of plants – submerged, floating and emergent – and your garden pond should have representatives of all three groups if possible. Submerged species may thrust their flowers above the surface but they remain underwater for the most part, providing the pond with much of its oxygen. Hornwort, Canadian waterweed and water milfoil are among the best of these oxygenators. Just throw a few pieces into your garden pond and they will quickly produce dense clumps of vegetation. Water violet – not a true violet but a member of the primrose family – is also well worth growing for its spikes of delicate, violet-coloured flowers.

Best known of the floating plants are, of course, the water lilies. You can grow cultivated forms as well as our native yellow and white species; all provide nectar for insects, and their leaves make good perches for dragonflies and frogs.

ABOVE: A rich mixture of marginal and floating plants gives this pond a balanced and natural appearance. The nearby trees are far enough away not to cast heavy shade on the water.

Water lilies are best grown in the deepest part of the pond, planted in plastic baskets weighted down with stones. The fringed water lily, a member of the bogbean family, is a much more delicate plant, worth trying in the shallower parts of the pond, together with amphibious bistort. Both produce attractive flowers.

Duckweed, the smallest of all the flowering plants, will arrive in your pond sooner or later. Small patches can be quite attractive, but don't let it cover the surface and cut off the light from the submerged plants. Keep all your floating plants in check, and ideally try to keep about half of the surface area free of vegetation so that it will attract dragonflies and other aquatic insects (see page 120).

EMERGENT PLANTS

These provide nectar for visiting insects and also essential cover for amphibians and other creatures moving in and out of the water. If you examine them early on summer mornings you might well see dragonfly nymphs crawling up them in readiness for the dramatic change to the adult stage. More often, however, you will just find the empty skins – evidence that the transformation has already taken place. Good emergent plants include: flowering rush, arrowhead, bogbean, water mint (which you can use in the kitchen, although it is not as strong as garden mint), brooklime, water forget-me-not, lesser spearwort, yellow iris and purple loosestrife.

These are all best planted in baskets on the marginal shelf or in the shallows. They can be obtained from most good garden or aquatic centres, or can be scrounged from other pond-owners. Never take them from the wild.

Above right: Flowering rush

Right: Bogbean

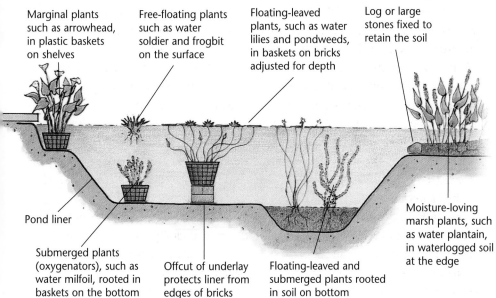

Marginal plants such as arrowhead, in plastic baskets on shelves

Free-floating plants such as water soldier and frogbit on the surface

Floating-leaved plants, such as water lilies and pondweeds, in baskets on bricks adjusted for depth

Log or large stones fixed to retain the soil

Pond liner

Submerged plants (oxygenators), such as water milfoil, rooted in baskets on the bottom

Offcut of underlay protects liner from edges of bricks

Floating-leaved and submerged plants rooted in soil on bottom

Moisture-loving marsh plants, such as water plantain, in waterlogged soil at the edge

Left: *This shows how a pond and marginal marsh can be constructed with a flexible liner, and also demonstrates how some submerged and marginal plants can be planted.*

Pond-dwellers

FAR RIGHT: Pond snails, like the one seen here gliding on the underside of the water surface, can be useful for controlling green algae, but if you have too many in your pond, they may eat the plants as well.

The pond-dwellers fall into three main ecological groups: the free-swimming creatures, including beetles and bugs, fishes, and assorted small crustaceans; the crawlers, such as worms and snails and a variety of young insects; and the surface-dwelling pond skaters and whirligig beetles. The water surface behaves as if it has a thin skin, and if you look carefully at the pond skaters you will see the little dimples made by their water-repellent feet. A fourth group of animals associated with the pond are the birds that come to bathe and drink there.

Most animals will find their way to your pond by themselves, but it is still a good idea to 'seed' a new pond with a few bucketfuls of water taken from an existing pond, or even a water butt. This will help

to introduce some of the microscopic organisms on which most other pond life depends. Diving beetles, pond skaters, water boatmen, dragonflies, mayflies and mosquitoes will not take long to arrive. Although you might not welcome the mosquitoes, the dragonflies and birds

RIGHT: Newts are some of the easiest pond creatures to watch. Like most amphibians, they live partly in the water and partly on land, but they tend to be more aquatic than the frogs and toads.

FAR LEFT: *Pond skaters skim rapidly over the pond surface on their long, water-repellent legs in search of other insects that fall into the water.*

LEFT: *The red-eyed damselfly likes well-vegetated ponds and often rests on water lily leaves. The female lacks the blue patch at the rear.*

certainly will (see page 12). Many other small creatures will probably arrive on the plants that you put in the pond.

Frogs and newts quickly discover new ponds, but toads are less likely to arrive under their own steam because they normally return to the ponds where they grew up. Scrounge a bit of spawn or some tadpoles from a neighbour's pond if you want to have some toads. However, avoid the temptation to put fish in anything

but a large pond because they will eat many of the other animals! However, don't be surprised to find some small fishes in your pond anyway; eggs can arrive with the plants you introduce and even on the feet of visiting birds.

BELOW: *Bathing helps birds to remove dirt and parasites. Make sure your pond has a shallow end or a log or some boulders on which the birds can perform their ablutions.*

A log garden

The woodland floor is a surprisingly rich habitat where fungi and a host of small animals break down and recycle the dead wood and leaves. Without these vital organisms, the human race would have been buried under a mountain of dead wood long ago: in fact, we would probably never have evolved.

It is quite easy to create a replica of the woodland floor to house some of these fascinating creatures in a shady corner of your garden. All you need is a few logs stacked up with plenty of gaps between them, but you can make a more attractive feature by surrounding the stack with a bed of wood or bark chippings. Spray the logs occasionally with water in dry weather, because the resident plants and animals do not like to get too dry.

Wildlife inhabitants

Dead wood in the forest is the natural home of the furniture beetle (woodworm) and other timber pests, and these insects are among the first to attack your logs. As the timber softens, they may be followed by stag beetles and the much more common lesser stag beetles, whose fat, juicy grubs tunnel through the timber for several years. *Endomychus coccineus* is a ladybird look-alike that feeds on fungal threads under the bark. Woodlice and millipedes live under loose bark and eat the timber softened by the fungi. Centipedes, spiders and ground beetles

> **CONSERVATION TIP**
>
> Do not construct your log garden close to old or valuable trees. Honey fungus may well invade the logs and it could spread to living trees. Although it rarely harms young, healthy trees, older specimens are sometimes killed by the fungus.

RIGHT AND FAR RIGHT:

The antlers of the male stag beetle (right) are much enlarged jaws and they are used to fight over the females. The latter have much smaller jaws and look more like the lesser stag beetle (far right), although they are not as black.

hunt in and around the logs, and many other invertebrates find their food and shelter there. Don't be afraid to lift a log occasionally to see what is lurking beneath.

Wrens love to hunt insects and spiders in the log garden, while hedgehogs, mice and voles often make their homes there. Little piles of grain and other fruits or seeds hidden among the logs are sure signs that mice or voles are in residence.

LEFT: *Toadstools most often appear on logs in the autumn. A cluster like this can scatter millions of spores, but very few will reach a suitable spot in which to grow.*

GARDEN PROJECT – CREATING A LOG GARDEN

Use logs of varying thicknesses in your log garden, and try to get wood of several different species – oak, beech, ash, elm and pine, for example. This will increase the variety of insects and other creatures attracted to it, and you can then watch the gradual disintegration of the timber over several years as a succession of fungi and other organisms move in.

Mosses and lichens may already be growing on the bark when you get the logs. Although they don't do much towards breaking down the timber, they do act as nurseries for ferns and other plants whose roots get under the bark and open the way for animal life.

The toadstools and bracket fungi that may sprout from the logs are just the reproductive parts that scatter the spores. Most of the fungus consists of hair-like threads which spread through the timber and soften it by exuding digestive juices. Some species attack solid timber soon after it has fallen, but others prefer to wait until it has been softened by the earlier invaders.

It is a good idea to add fresh logs and wood chips to your log garden from time to time so that you always have timber in various stages of decay. The completely rotted material can then be spread on the rest of your garden.

LEFT: *When building your log garden, don't forget to leave a few gaps for the mice and hedgehogs to get in. Solitary bees and wasps (see page 116) are quite likely to tunnel into the softer logs.*

Under your feet

The soil that supports your garden plants is an extremely complex material, the make-up of which varies with the nature of the underlying rocks. These rocks provide the bulk of the soil's mineral content, sometimes known as the soil skeleton. However, a mature soil also has a significant organic content which is derived from the many organisms that live and die in it.

With a wildlife population ranging from the microscopic bacteria that play a vital role in recycling the nutrients, through worms and other creep-crawlies to moles, your soil is a living community. Forget this and your garden will suffer.

Indispensable earthworms

Most gardeners take little notice of the worms that are brought up with almost every forkful of soil. However, Charles Darwin reckoned the earthworm to be the most important animal in the history of the world. A 1000 m² plot of good garden loam may support 25,000 worms which, by pushing and chewing their way through the soil, can create up to 5 km (3 miles) of new tunnels each day! Although the individual tunnels may not last very long, they do play a major role in draining and aerating the soil – and Darwin realized this is vital for the well-being of plant roots. Worms also enrich the soil by dragging dead leaves into it and bringing mineral-rich material up to the surface layers where

RIGHT: Watch worms at work by making a simple wormery with two glass sheets separated by a length of stout rope and held in place by bulldog clips. Fill the wormery with layers of garden soil, sand and potting compost, and put some dead leaves on the surface. Water well and add four or five worms. Put the wormery in a black polythene bag. After a day or so you will find the soil layers mixed and the leaves dragged into the worms' tunnels.

it can be used by plant roots. The alkaline nature of worm-casts promotes the growth of certain vitamin-secreting bacteria, and the vitamin improves root growth and crop yield. Be aware of this if you are tempted to use a worm-killer on your lawn. A healthy soil is surely worth a few worm-casts.

Remember also that treating your flowers and vegetables to organic manure is far better for the worms than spraying them with chemical fertilizers. Worms feed on organic matter and you have

only to look in your compost heap to see how well they flourish when surrounded by rotting vegetation.

LEFT: Half in and half out of their burrows, these earthworms snuggle up and dig their bristles into each other before they exchange sperm. Each worm then withdraws into its own burrow and lays its eggs. Earthworms are hermaphrodite with both male and female organs in each individual.

BELOW: *Centipedes are often mistakenly called 'wireworms'. Numerous joints enable them to bend their bodies in any direction.*

Slugs that eat earthworms

Slugs are often described as snails without shells, but a few slugs do have a tiny shell, perched on the rear end of the body and looking like a little finger nail. These tapering, yellowish slugs spend most of their time under the ground, where they feed entirely on earthworms. The slug shoots out its spiky tongue to impale a passing worm and then sucks it in like a piece of spaghetti.

LEFT: *You might unearth one of these shelled slugs while you are turning over the vegetable patch, but you are more likely to find them under large stones or paving slabs that have not been disturbed for a while.*

The compost heap

Every garden should have a compost heap where kitchen and garden waste can be converted to valuable plant food. As well as enabling you to enrich your soil for free, composting your organic rubbish helps the whole environment by reducing the amount of material going to land-fill sites.

In our throw-away society, the demand for land-fill sites is increasing all the time and many natural habitats are in the firing line, so anything you can do to reduce the quantity of material going into your dustbin will help. Use recycling centres for glass, metal and paper, and compost the rest of your organic rubbish instead of buying peat. If you have no space in your garden you can use a composting bin. Some local councils provide these cheaply or even free of charge in order to reduce the amount of garbage they have to collect.

ABOVE: *The brandling worm, which is easily recognized by its bold rings, is the commonest earthworm in most compost heaps.*

What to compost

Any organic material can be composted – even a railway sleeper will eventually rot away – but typical materials for the heap include dead leaves, grass cuttings, hedge clippings (preferably shredded), weeds, potato peelings and tea bags. It is a good idea to build your heap on a layer of twigs, as this will let air into the base. Bacteria will soon get to work on the material, producing heat that steps up the rate of decay. Surrounding the heap with some wooden planks or sheets of corrugated iron will help to keep in the warmth, as does covering it with an old piece of carpet. The rate of conversion to compost depends on the temperature and the type of material in the heap, but you can speed it up by adding the odd bucket of horse manure or an occasional sprinkling of nitrogenous fertilizer to encourage bacterial growth.

RIGHT: *Cryptops is a blind but very active centipede with 21 pairs of legs. The last pair are very stout and act like extra antennae.*

ABOVE: *Woodlice are mainly nocturnal and tend to huddle together in damp places during the day. Two species are resting on this piece of wood lifted from a compost heap.*

Teeming with wildlife

While providing free food for your garden plants, your compost heap is also a happy hunting ground for numerous animals. Arriving in various ways, many of them play a major role in the breakdown and eventual decay of the material. Feeding on smaller creatures or on the rotting vegetation itself, they range from microscopic mites to hedgehogs. When you are turning the heap or digging out the compost, start gently to reduce the risk of spearing any dozing hedgehogs with your fork (see page 49).

The smaller animals are not evenly distributed through the compost. Brandling worms like the moister parts and abound in layers of grass clippings or dead leaves, whereas woodlice and some centipedes prefer slightly drier parts of the heap and scurry around when you disturb the material. Slugs and snails wander all over the heap at night or after rain, and it is worth looking out for the extraordinary aerial courtship of the great grey or leopard slug. Up to 15 cm (6 in) long, the slugs meet in the compost and then, after a prolonged slimy embrace, they climb a fence post or other vertical surface. Tightly entwined, they then lower themselves on a rope of mucus and mating finally takes place in mid-air, often a metre or two above the ground and well out of the reach of marauding hedgehogs! On returning to the ground, each slug goes off and lays its eggs; slugs are hermaphrodite creatures with both male and female organs in each individual.

The smallest wildlife

If you want to see the smaller inhabitants of your compost heap, spread out a handful of compost on a white surface and examine it with a magnifying glass. Grotesque mites mingle with tiny beetles, while springtails leap into the air at the slightest disturbance. The droppings of all these tiny animals make up a high proportion of the older and more decayed compost. The predatory false scorpions possess some of the animal kingdom's most potent venom but luckily are too small to hurt us. They usually arrive in the heap by hitching lifts on flies and other insects, to which they cling with their relatively huge pincers.

ABOVE: *Entwined great grey slugs extrude their genitalia to exchange sperm while hanging from a fence post.*

LEFT: *The pincers look threatening and usually carry a powerful venom, but the false scorpion is no more than 4 mm long.*

PART TWO

Garden Mammals

Our garden mammals are warm-blooded animals with fur coats. About 30 species might visit a rural garden from time to time, but fewer are likely to take up permanent residence. Represented by herbivorous, carnivorous and omnivorous species, they range in size from tiny shrews and bats to deer. Most of them will come into your garden whether you like it or not, although you may not be aware of them because they are generally nocturnal and rather quiet. Apart from deer and squirrels, which can damage trees and shrubs, most of these visitors are pretty harmless. Hedgehogs do a lot of good by eating harmful slugs and other pests, so it's worth encouraging them into your garden.

There can be few gardens that don't receive visits from domestic cats and, being carnivorous creatures, they inevitably kill and eat quite a lot of our garden wildlife. It has been estimated that British cats kill 275 million birds and other small animals each year and, although there is no hard and fast evidence that cats have been responsible for a decline in garden bird populations, they do not have a beneficial effect. So keep your cat well-fed so it has less interest in wildlife, and fit a bell or a sonic collar to warn birds of its presence. If you are bothered by cats from elsewhere, avoid putting any bird food on the ground.

Reading the signs

Most of our mammals are nocturnal so it is not easy to see them going about their business. However, they leave plenty of clues in the form of footprints, food remains and droppings, and with a bit of detective work you can usually find out which mammals visit your garden at night.

Tell-tale footprints

One easy way to discover which animals explore your garden during the night is to put down a patch of damp soft sand and look for footprints in the morning. You can encourage the animals to walk over the sand by leaving various foods in the middle.

ABOVE: *A badger's footprint is easily identified by its breadth and by the long, chunky impressions of its toes – usually five, although the inner toe does not always leave a mark.*

Bread flavoured with aniseed is said to be especially attractive to mice and other small mammals, and you can also try fruit, sliced carrot, grain and a portion of pet food. These should attract a variety of wildlife which will leave plenty of tracks for you to interpret. Even beetles and earwigs leave footprints if the ground is soft enough.

Another way to detect the presence of small mammals is to put some bait in the centre of a sheet of paper that has been smoked over a candle. Little feet pick up the smoke particles and leave clear tracks.

ABOVE: *Footprints are easy to spot and follow in the snow, although they are usually less clear than on muddy ground. This is the print or slot of a roe deer, up to 5 cm (2 in) long.*

Hairy evidence

Larger mammals, including badgers and deer, often leave hairs behind when they brush against thorny bushes or pass through or under wire fences. It is usually possible to identify the hairs. The long outer hairs of the badger, for example, are dark in the centre and pale at the base and the tip. Because these animals tend to tread regular pathways, finding tufts of hair will show you where to watch for them at night. If you can't see the spot from the house or the garden shed, try rigging up a simple hide. An old, dark curtain hung on a bamboo frame can be quite effective if you cut small holes for your torch and binoculars. The animals do not like bright lights and you are less likely to alarm them if you cover your torch with a piece of red plastic. Of

course, image intensifiers or infra-red binoculars are the ideal equipment, but these are much too expensive for most garden-watchers.

'SQUIRRELED' PINE CONES

Pine conesstripped like this indicate that squirrels have been busy. Mice make a neater job of removing the cone scales.

HOW TO CRACK A NUT

Hazel nuts are eagerly sought by many birds and mammals and each species has its own way of opening them. Look for the opened nuts under a hazel tree if you have one. Alternatively, scatter some nuts on the ground and wait for them to be opened – but don't be surprised if most of them are taken away for opening and eating. Nuthatches and woodpeckers, for example, wedge the nuts into bark crevices and hammer them open.

A squirrel splits a hazel nut cleanly in half by nibbling a little hole at the top and then using its lower front teeth to prise the two halves apart.

The bank vole gnaws a neat hole either in the top or at the side of the nut, leaving an extremely clean edge on the outer surface of the nut.

The wood mouse gnaws a hole in the side of the nut but it always leave a distinctive ring of tooth marks around the outside of the hole.

Hedgehogs

The prickly hedgehog is probably the most familiar and engaging of our nocturnal mammalian visitors. It is certainly the easiest one to watch as it trundles across the lawn in search of worms, beetles and other tasty morsels on a summer evening.

The hedgehog's eyesight is not brilliant and you can usually get quite close to it; you don't even need a red filter on your torch. The animal may roll into a spiky ball if you make sudden movements or sounds, but it is just as likely to sit quietly and stare back at you. However, if you take your eyes off it for just a moment, it will probably disappear without a sound; it is remarkably quick for an animal with short legs.

On the other hand, the hedgehog can be extremely noisy, especially when scratching for food in the hedge bottom or the herbaceous border: it is not called the hedgepig for nothing. Courtship is also a noisy and very public affair, with much grunting and squealing as the pair leap around each other on the lawn.

Hedgehog dinner

Hedgehogs often eat birds' eggs and occasionally catch mice and frogs and even snakes, but invertebrates are their favourite food. Examination of their sausage-shaped droppings will reveal a high proportion of beetle remains. Caterpillars and earthworms are equally important, although they contain fewer indigestible remains. Garden hedgehogs will always appreciate some extra food, and a saucer of mealworms is likely to attract several animals. They are equally happy with a plate of dog food, garnished with some sliced apple or dried fruit.

BELOW: *The hedgehog's spiky armour is formed from modified hairs. Although effective against most predators, it does make grooming difficult and hedgehogs are usually well endowed with fleas!*

CONSERVATION TIP

If you find a baby hedgehog in the garden after the middle of September, try to catch it and stick it on your kitchen scales. If it weighs less than about 450 g (1 lb) it is unlikely to survive the winter in the wild, as it will not have enough fat on it. Take it in and feed it up, remembering to dust it with flea powder! Once it has reached 500 g (1 lb 2 oz) or so, you can release it or keep it indoors through the winter. It won't bother about hibernation if you keep it warm.

Bread and milk has long been the traditional snack for hedgehogs but, although nourishing, it should not be given too often because, like us, hedgehogs need a balanced diet. Extra food is very valuable in dry summer weather when worms and other creepy-crawlies burrow down out of reach, and also in autumn when the hedgehogs are preparing for their winter sleep. Additional food at such times can save their lives.

Winter quarters

As the days shorten in the autumn, the hedgehogs fatten themselves up and search out suitable sleeping quarters – often in a hedge bottom, a log pile or a compost heap. Each animal busies itself gathering dead leaves and then packing them into a recess to form a ball up to 50 cm (20 in) in diameter. The hedgehog then burrows into it and settles down for the winter.

If you are any good at sticking bits of wood together you can help your garden hedgehogs by making them a box with a hedgehog-sized opening. Fill it with leaves and shove it into your compost heap. Alternatively, simply cover it with branches – a good use for leylandii trimmings perhaps – and one of the local hedgehogs will be more than happy to move in. If you are no good at working with wood, you can buy hedgehog homes at garden centres and pet shops.

LEFT: *Garden hedgehogs readily nest in boxes like this during the summer. Put the box in a secluded spot, half-fill it with leaves and then cover it with a sack or some branches. Do not use straw or hay as bedding as the sharp stems can cause injuries.*

BELOW: *Hedgehog courtship, which can be witnessed through the summer, usually starts with the male trotting round and round the female and snorting loudly.*

Rodents

With about 1,700 species, the rodents are the largest of all the groups of mammals. Characterized by continuously-growing, chisel-like front teeth that can gnaw through almost anything, they include rats and mice, voles, squirrels and beavers.

Mice

Although not the most welcome of garden guests, because of their liking for newly-sown peas and other vegetables, these little mammals can be amusing to watch and, of course, they attract a number of equally fascinating predators, including stoats, weasels and kestrels. I doubt if there is a garden anywhere without a few mice and voles, but they rarely show themselves and you will have to give them a bit of encouragement if you want to watch them.

The woodmouse is the mouse most likely to be seen in the garden. Look for its bulging eyes and very large ears. It lives in hedgerows and compost heaps, in the woodpile or under the garden shed. The house mouse has smaller eyes than the woodmouse and lacks the white belly. It normally stays close to houses and sheds.

Voles

A vole has a shorter and blunter snout than a mouse and its tiny ears are almost hidden in its fur. The bank vole, which is identified by its reddish-brown fur, is common in many rural gardens, where it forages in hedge bottoms and shrubberies. It also climbs well and is not averse to a meal of raspberries and other soft fruits. The much duller field vole likes more open areas with long grass, including

ABOVE: *Its large eyes and huge ears indicate that the wood mouse is essentially a nocturnal creature. It is hardly ever seen by day.*

ABOVE: *The bank vole is active by day and night. It eats some worms and insects, but it is largely vegetarian and seeds are its main food.*

LEFT: *This little field vole exhibits the typically blunt snout and small eyes of the voles. Almost entirely vegetarian, it is most active at dusk and dawn.*

orchards. If you have room to lay down some corrugated sheets you might well find field voles nesting under them.

The garden dormouse

Although absent from Britain, the garden dormouse is widely distributed through Western Europe and is one of the most attractive garden visitors. A little smaller than a rat, it is readily distinguished by the bushy black and white tip to its tail and the black 'mask' enclosing its eyes and the base of each ear. Easily lured with nuts and fruit, sometimes it will take up residence in boxes intended for birds. Like the closely related glis-glis (see page 52), it often gets into houses and makes a lot of noise when scampering around the loft at night. It can also produce considerable mess with its droppings and is not averse to hibernating in the spare room!

NOSY SHREWS

Shrews are commonly confused with mice, but they are readily distinguished by their long, slender snout and tiny ears. They are not rodents but belong to the same group as the hedgehog and the mole. Shrews hunt for worms and other creepy-crawlies in the hedgerows and long grass by day and night, but rarely break cover.

WILDLIFE PROJECT – BUILDING A MOUSE TABLE

Just as birds come to your bird table, so mice and voles can be persuaded to visit a 'mouse table'. You need some kind of board, roughly 50 cm (20 in) square, although the dimensions do not matter much, and some wire netting to make a cage over it. Netting with holes no more than 2.5 cm (1 in) across will allow the mice and voles to get in but will keep out most of their enemies, including cats and rats. Almost any kind of food will attract your guests, but peanut butter, chocolate, dried fruit and breakfast cereal are among the best. Make the cage about 50 cm (20 in) high and include some small branches, giving the animals somewhere to 'play' and make themselves more visible to you. Set up the table where you can see it easily, with or without binoculars – not too close to your vegetable patch! Use a torch with a red filter at first, but the animals will soon get used to ordinary light. Voles may even visit the mouse table in daylight.

The glis-glis

Also called the edible dormouse, the glis-glis is easily mistaken for a small grey squirrel, but it can be distinguished by the dark ring round each eye. Although it is widely distributed across the European continent, in Britain it is restricted to a small area of the Chilterns where it was introduced about 100 years ago. A very sociable creature, it commonly invades outbuildings and roof cavities. Make sure your apple store is securely closed for it will do almost anything for an apple.

Squirrels

These are the most obvious rodents in many gardens, especially those with trees. The red squirrel occurs on the European mainland, but the somewhat larger grey squirrel – introduced from North America – is the only one found in most parts of England and Wales. The animals quickly learn to take peanuts (unsalted) from your hand,

and it is fun to watch them stripping pine and spruce cones to obtain the seeds, but they can be a nuisance at the bird table. Few of the so-called squirrel-proof feeding devices defeat these intelligent creatures for long. As well as eating nuts and other seeds, they strip bark, eat fungi and dig up bulbs and corms; in the spring they eat birds' eggs and nestlings. So it is not a brilliant idea to encourage squirrels into your garden.

ABOVE: *The red squirrel's prominent ear-tufts develop in autumn, but gradually wear away in the winter and are absent in the summer.*

RIGHT: *Grey squirrels quickly become tame in parks and gardens where they are fed regularly, but feeding these animals is not encouraged!*

Deer

Beautiful as they are, deer are not usually welcome in our gardens because they see most of our plants as food. There are probably more deer in Britain now than at any time since the Middle Ages.

Gardens close to woodland may be visited by fallow deer, but otherwise you are likely to see only muntjac and roe deer. Both species can push their way through poorly-maintained hedges, and roe deer can also leap over low gates and fences. Their characteristic footprints, known as slots (see page 46), will show you where they get in. Shrubberies and rose beds are common targets for these browsing deer, but they will also dine on your vegetables in spring and early summer.

LEFT: *Although often seen by day in the summer, roe deer are active mainly at dusk and dawn. Look for the black nose and the pale rump. The animals are about 65 cm (26 in) high at the shoulder and, as with other deer, only the males have antlers.*

LEFT: *Muntjac feed by day and night, although they are most active at dusk and dawn. They are about 50 cm (20 in) high at the shoulder and the male's antlers are a mere 6–8 cm (2–3 in) long. Its barking calls give this animal its alternative name of barking deer. Introduced from China, it is now widespread in southern England.*

Foxes

You will always know if a fox has wandered through your garden at night because it leaves its characteristic smell everywhere. It is difficult to describe this odour, but it resembles that of the weed herb robert.

The best way to learn what reynard smells like is to go for a walk with someone who already knows the odour, or to go to a zoo or wildlife park and have a good sniff; then you will always recognize the strong, musky scent when you encounter it.

Foxes are extremely common, even in towns: in fact, they are more widespread in many urban areas than they are in the countryside. They are real scavengers and obtain a lot of their food from dustbins. Although few people are prepared to encourage foxes into their gardens, it is very easy to attract them to a plate of dog food placed on the lawn at night (as long as the neighbourhood cats do not get there first). Use red torchlight to watch from your window and, with a bit of luck, you will be able to see what a handsome creature the fox is. It might scratch around for worms, but otherwise it will do no harm in your garden as long as you lock up your chickens and other livestock – foxes do not carry keys!

RIGHT: *Foxes are essentially solitary creatures, but two or three may gather where food is put out regularly.*

Badgers

Although not many people can claim ever to have seen a badger, these heavily-built nocturnal creatures are really quite common wherever areas of deciduous woodland are interspersed with open country.

Badgers emerge from their sets in the evening and may cover several kilometres as they search out a variety of plant and animal food. They frequently visit railway embankments and cemeteries, and if your garden is close to deciduous woodland the chances are that you will be able to attract them with a dish of dog food and some table scraps. If the food is put out regularly, any badgers that find it will soon include your garden in their nightly rounds and become regular visitors.

I know a pub that used to make a fortune by feeding badgers in a corner of the garden. Customers would sit there every evening and eat and drink their way through large quantities of crisps and beer as they watched the animals! The badgers soon got used to being watched; even the strong lights did not worry or deter them.

Badgers are fond of earthworms and may pull your compost heap to pieces in search of them. They occasionally dig up the lawn in search of moles, but you can usually divert their attention with other food. It is exciting to see them materialize silently out of the twilight, and the enjoyment you get from watching them surely outweighs any damage that they might do in your garden.

ABOVE: *The bold black and white stripes on the head may help badgers to recognize each other at night, or they may be a warning to other animals.*

LEFT: *Although badgers live in communities, they usually tend to forage by themselves, but, like foxes, they will feed together where food is provided. Tempt them with fruit as well as meaty foods.*

Bats

Most gardens, even those in the middle of towns, are visited by bats at night. You will often see them circling street lamps at high speed to snap up the moths and other insects that are drawn to the light.

Although we cannot hear them, bats continually emit high-frequency sounds, which are way above our hearing range, and use the echoes to detect their insect prey. This echo-location also enables the bats to avoid obstacles, so you need have no fear that they will bump into you.

Of the 16 bat species in Britain, only three are commonly seen over gardens: the common pipistrelle, the much larger serotine and the brown long-eared bat. The common pipistrelle is the one that we normally see swooping around the garden at a height of 2–3 m (6–9 ft). It is also Britain's smallest bat, weighing no more than about 8 g (¹⁄₄ oz) although it has a wingspan of about 25 cm (10 in).

Bat homes

Most bats are associated with hollow trees, caves and elderly buildings, and the loss or 'improvement' of such sites has undoubtedly led to the decline of several species. The tiny pipistrelle bat can find plenty of roosting sites, even in modern houses, but it still appreciates some additional accommodation. A rough board or a couple of planks screwed to a pair of vertical battens will provide a fine summer roosting place if fixed just under the eaves on a south- or west-facing house wall, and then you may be able to enjoy the sight of the bats streaming out to feed at dusk. Pipistrelles are sociable creatures

ABOVE: *The long-eared bat flies quite slowly, usually close to trees, and snatches insects from the leaves. You can attract it to your garden with a dish of mealworms.*

ABOVE: *Although they use echo-location to navigate and find their food, the bats are not really blind, but you will have to look hard to spot the eyes of this pipistrelle bat.*

This is a simple wall-mounted bat roost. The slit opening at the bottom should be no more than 2 cm (^{3}/$_4$ in) wide. Fixed to a north-facing wall, it might be used as a winter roost. Do not treat the timber with any kind of preservative as most of these are poisonous to bats.

ABOVE: *The grooves on the back wall of this box will give the bats a better grip as they go in and out.*

ABOVE: *Schwegler boxes, made from wood and cement, provide excellent insulation and make ideal homes for bats. Fix them to tree trunks in pairs, one on each side of the trunk, so that the bats can move if they get too hot.*

Bat rescue

Baby bats start to fly as young as three or four weeks old, but they are not very good at it initially and many fall to the ground beneath the roost. Unable to get airborne again, most of them quickly perish, so it is worth trying to return them to the roost. Alternatively, keep them warm indoors and feed them with skimmed milk and crushed mealworms (see page 64) until they are strong enough to fly. Release them from an upstairs window at dusk.

and 50 or more individuals may use such a roost, but don't expect it to be occupied right away. Pipistrelles also have a touch of gypsy in them, so do not be surprised if they use the roost you have provided for a while and then move away. You can find out if your roost is occupied by putting a plank of wood on the ground beneath it: if bats are in residence you will find droppings on the wood.

PART THREE

Garden Birds

I doubt if there is a garden anywhere that does not have some bird life: even the barest town garden has a few house sparrows searching for crumbs. I can't imagine a garden without birds. They may pull our crocuses to pieces in the spring and pinch our currants in the summer but they give us an immense amount of pleasure and are the most popular of our garden guests.

Robins, house sparrows and many other common garden birds are with us throughout the year, but we also get summer visitors from Africa. These are mostly insect-eaters, such as swallows, house martins and spotted flycatchers, making the most of our flies and midges. Residents and summer visitors may nest in our gardens if we provide the right vegetation or nest boxes, although most of the birds we see are just passing through.

We also get winter visitors, including fieldfares and redwings, from northern Europe. Although the birds are warm-blooded and have a good covering of feathers, they can't survive the winter in the far north because they cannot find enough food under the snow or in the frozen ground. Along with our resident birds, they brighten any garden and appreciate the food we put out for them. Our gardens certainly would not be the same without them.

A beak for the job

Few birds regularly eat twigs and leaves, but otherwise they have evolved the ability to deal with virtually every kind of food on offer, from minute seeds and insects, through fruits of all kinds, to fish, flesh and carrion.

If you have a pond that attracts herons and perhaps kingfishers, you can watch the birds going through the whole menu in your garden, and it will become very obvious that each species of bird has its preferred kind of food. For example, you will not see swallows dragging worms from the lawn, blackbirds streaking across the sky to snatch insects in full flight, or herons digging their beaks into fallen apples. And you don't need a degree in ornithology to appreciate that each bird's beak or bill is beautifully adapted for its diet and the chosen task.

Beak shapes

The members of each family usually have similar diets, and therefore similar beaks, although there are plenty of exceptions to this rule. Finch beaks, for example, range from the tiny tweezer-like apparatus of the goldfinch to the hawfinch's 'sledge-hammer', able to crack cherry stones, and the peculiar scissor-like beak with which the crossbill slices into pine and spruce cones. Although all these birds are seed-eaters, they avoid competing with each other by specializing in different kinds of seeds.

On the level

Blue tits and great tits eat the same kinds of food but avoid serious competition by foraging at different levels – blue tits mainly in tree branches and great tits on or near the ground. If they did not divide up the food source in this way the great tit would slowly wipe out the smaller blue tit. Swallows and house martins similarly

LEFT: *The chaffinch's beak is not very highly specialized and can cope with a fairly wide range of foods. It is stout enough and sufficiently strong to crack many seeds, but at the same time dainty enough to be able to peck insects from bark crevices.*

ABOVE: *The wren specializes in insects and spiders. Its slender beak can pick them up easily and has no trouble in crushing their soft bodies.*

share out the available food by hunting at different levels – the swallows usually feeding within about 30 m (90 ft) of the ground while the house martins are most likely to be seen above 50 m (150 ft).

It is important to remember the different dietary preferences of birds when feeding them in the garden. Don't expect all your visitors to be content with bread crumbs and the occasional treat of peanuts. The greater the variety of food you can provide, the larger will be your reward in terms of the number of bird species visiting your garden.

Multi-purpose beaks

Birds also use their beaks with amazing dexterity to build their nests. It's not easy to watch birds building their nests – and it is illegal to disturb them – but it can be almost as intriguing to watch them gathering nesting materials beforehand.

ABOVE: *Woodpeckers use their powerful beaks like chisels to dig for insects in tree trunks, although the green woodpecker (pictured here) is more likely to feed on ants on the ground. The birds also use their beaks to excavate nest holes in trees.*

Food for the birds

Birds can usually find plenty to eat by foraging in the garden, especially one with a good mix of habitats, but you can make life easier for them – and more fun for yourself – by providing them with additional food. They will soon get to know when and where to expect their meals, and their meal-time antics will be ample reward for a modest outlay on food.

The bird table

Many birds are happy to pick up the food that you scatter on the ground. Indeed, blackbirds and dunnocks prefer to take their meals on the ground, but where most species are concerned a table will benefit both the birds and bird-watcher. The table does not have to be elaborate: a simple tray about 50 cm (20 in) square and equipped with a rim and a few drainage holes is perfectly adequate. A roof is certainly not necessary.

The table should ideally be fixed to the top of a smooth metal pole about 2 m (6 ft) high. This should put it out of reach of any predatory cats and make it relatively safe from squirrels, although complete protection from squirrels is very difficult to achieve. If you have no secure spot for a pole-mounted table, you could fix one to a wall. Hanging one from a rope tied to two trees will keep it safe from cats, but not from squirrels. The table should be no more than 2 m (6 ft) from cover so that the birds can dart for safety if a sparrowhawk or

RIGHT: *A roof may actually deter some birds, but not these starlings, which often arrive in gangs and chase smaller birds away.*

another danger should present itself but, on the other hand, the cover should not be close enough to afford shelter to the cat!

You obviously need to be able to see the table clearly from a window, so don't site it where it will be in deep shade. The north side of the house is best, as the birds will not be silhouetted against the sun for much of the day. This is very important if you want to photograph your feathered visitors.

Suggested food

◆ **Left-overs** Scraps from your own meals will be appreciated by many birds, although they are not keen on vegetables other than potatoes. Fat trimmed from bacon and other meat before cooking is a good source of energy, and most birds also enjoy scraps of uncooked pastry.

◆ **Bird pudding** The above foods can be offered as they are, but a more interesting way of serving them is to make them into a special bird pudding or bird cake by adding them to a bowl of melted lard or dripping.

Breakfast cereals, including uncooked porridge oats, can also be added, together with crushed peanuts and other seeds, dried fruit and grated cheese. When set, the pudding can be dished up in various ways. It can be turned out and placed on the bird table in a solid mass, around which the birds can sit and feast for as long as they like, or you can pack it into a small flower pot or half a coconut shell and hang it upside-down for the tits to enjoy. You can also plaster the mixture into bark crevices, but I don't recommend this

other than in very cold weather because the fat will melt and leave some ugly marks on the trees.

◆ Bones from the weekend joint

Hang these up to attract tits and starlings. Even the robin will try to grab morsels of meat, although it is more likely to wait on the ground for the other birds to drop pieces. Be sure to remove the bones after two or three days to prevent the build-up of potentially harmful bacteria.

LEFT: *Blue tits will amuse you as they dig out the peanuts or bird pudding from holes in a swaying log. Make sure you leave some footholds on the log.*

LEFT: *Tits are the main visitors to terra cotta bells like this. The bells can be filled time and time again with bird pudding, either purchased ready-made or cooked up in your kitchen. Remember to wash the bells before refilling them.*

◆ **Seeds and dried fruit** Many birds will enjoy bird pudding, but the finches and other seed-eaters will be even happier with a variety of seeds and dried fruit. Commercially produced mixtures for wild birds can be bought from garden centres, pet shops and by mail order. Most of these products contain a wide range of oil-rich seeds and thus cater for many species of birds. Avoid mixtures with a high proportion of cereal-based products as these will not provide enough energy for birds during cold weather.

If you have the time and the patience, you can collect your own seeds from teasels, plantains, dandelions and various other plants. If you dry them well and store them in a dry place they will remain in good condition for several months. The cones of pines and other conifers yield useful amounts of seed. You can also collect acorns, beechnuts and hazel nuts.

◆ **Sunflower seeds** With their high fat or oil content, these are excellent for many garden birds. Black seeds are particularly nutritious and their relatively thin husks mean that birds do not have to expend a lot of energy opening them. 'Sunflower hearts', from which the husks have been removed, save even more energy – and you won't have to sweep up the husks!

◆ **Peanuts** These are the most popular food for our garden birds. Out of their shells, they are traditionally presented in a net or a basket, but you can wedge them into holes drilled in small logs. Hang the logs in a tree and watch the tits and, if you're lucky, woodpeckers and nuthatches trying to dig them out.

JUICY MEALWORMS

Mealworms, which are the larvae of a sturdy black beetle, are especially good for feeding wrens, dunnocks, house sparrows and blackbirds – robins will do almost anything to get them (see page 71). The insects are best served up in a smooth-sided dish, from which they cannot escape. Obtainable from good pet shops, mealworms are very easy to keep in well-ventilated containers. Keep them dry and feed them on dry biscuits: rye crispbread is very acceptable to them. Be sure to keep the lid on the container: your robin will soon learn where the worms are kept and will scoff the lot if it gets the chance – even if you keep them indoors!

Peanuts in their shells can be threaded on to lengths of fine wire and suspended from branches. Great tits and finches soon discover what is inside the shells. Salt is bad for birds, so never put out salted peanuts.

◆ **Fresh coconut** This is another favourite food, best served in the shell. Cut the nuts in half and hang each half upside-down from a convenient support; blue tits and great tits will have a swinging time as they chip away at the flesh with their little beaks. Never give the birds desiccated coconut for it has a nasty habit of swelling up inside them.

Bird feeders

You can buy a range of bird feeders from pet shops and specialist dealers, including the RSPB (see page 126). Hung from trees or walls or attached to your bird table, they will hold and dispense peanuts and seed mixtures very efficiently. Some are even designed to keep out squirrels!

When to feed

It was once thought that birds should be given additional food only during the winter, but most ornithologists now recommend feeding them right through the year. Apart from encouraging the birds to stay in and around your garden,

this will undoubtedly improve their breeding success. Although nestlings are usually given their natural food, the adults are happy to eat the additional food that we supply, thereby freeing more natural food for the nestlings. Once you have started to feed your garden birds, keep it up and try to feed them at a fixed time each day. Otherwise, birds that have come to depend on you might hang around all day instead of going off to forage; this could be fatal in the winter.

LEFT: *Robins are very fond of bird pudding. Several commercial varieties are available, incorporating different seed mixtures and appealing to various birds. The fat gives them plenty of energy.*

FAR LEFT: *Greenfinches are enjoying a feast of seeds from the several 'serving hatches' in this popular feeder, which is also fairly squirrel-proof.*

LEFT: *The dome of this ingenious feeder can be moved up and down. In its lowest position, only the smallest birds can get at the food.*

Plants for birds

Most of our garden birds originally inhabited woodland clearings and margins, so our hedge-lined gardens, with their trees and shrubberies, are home from home for them. Trees and shrubs provide food, nesting sites and song posts from which the birds can defend their territories and advertise for mates. Even one small tree can be a useful addition to the garden, forming a tiny nature reserve.

Native plants

Many native trees are worthy of a place in a small garden, but do try to get seedlings or saplings from your own area. This should ensure that they grow well and should also eliminate any risk of contaminating the gene pool with alien genes. It is worth contacting your local Wildlife Trust: many nature reserves sell saplings that are removed during winter management work. If you have room for only one tree and your soil is fairly light, a silver birch could be the ideal choice. This graceful, quick-growing and hardy species is attractive in all seasons and has good autumn colour. Tits and other birds enjoy its abundant small seeds, and also do well on its huge insect population. The tree supports over 200 insect species in Britain alone. For damp soils, the common alder takes a lot of beating. It has a beautiful shape and, although it lacks autumn colour, the male catkins

RIGHT: *The coal tit, easily identified by the white patch on the back of its sooty black head, breeds mainly in coniferous woodland, but will scour a wide range of deciduous and evergreen garden trees for insects and spiders in the winter.*

give it a fine purple tinge in the winter. Its cone-like fruits yield a good supply of seeds for finches and other birds.

Other good trees include hazel, whose nuts attract plenty of birds and squirrels, bird cherry, rowan, crab apple, dogwood, guelder rose, buckthorn and spindle. The latter produces brilliant pink and orange fruits, but farmers don't like it much as it is a winter host of the infamous blackfly. Elder usually yields a fine crop of berries, loved by blackcaps and many other birds, but it is a scruffy tree and best relegated to an out-of-the-way corner. Its strong-smelling foliage deters many animals and only four British moths feed on it.

If you grow apples or pears, then leave some of the windfalls out for the birds. Blackbirds and starlings really like them, and if you keep some of the fruit back for the winter you might attract fieldfares and redwings as well. If you don't grow your own, try scrounging some 'tired' apples and other fruits from your local greengrocer. You can get them quite cheaply – for a song, you might say – and you will get plenty of bird-song in return.

Where to plant trees

Plant the trees in small clumps if you have room for more than one, and try to plant them on the north side. This will give your garden some protection from the coldest winds and provide a sheltered, sunny spot for some woodland-edge plants, such as bluebells and foxgloves. It will also create a sunny spot in which to sit and watch your garden visitors. You can scatter some chipped bark or leave a few logs under the trees to give the area a more natural look.

LEFT: *The guelder rose has large plates of fragrant cream flowers in early summer, followed by shiny red bird-friendly berries. The shrub does best on slightly damp soils.*

Trees and shrubs for nests

The trees I have mentioned above provide plenty of food for the birds but, although the collared dove may well be tempted to fix its flimsy platform to the branches, most birds prefer to nest in something a little more compact. Holly is good, especially if you plant a berry-bearing specimen that will provide food as well, and whitebeam is particularly good in town gardens. Hawthorn, blackthorn, firethorn, *Stranvaesia (Photinia) davidii*, *Rosa rugosa* and various cotoneasters are all worth planting, either as specimen shrubs or as part of a hedge. Don't be too eager to trim them and your reward will be a wealth of colourful autumnal fruits. In any case, do not trim the branches until the birds have finished nesting.

Useful climbers

Boston ivy, also known as Virginia creeper, is commonly grown on houses for its brilliant autumn colours. The dense

RIGHT: *Both the house sparrow, seen here, and the tree sparrow appreciate a good growth of ivy as a roosting site. Although essentially seed-eating birds, they happily snap up the tasty insects and spiders lurking among the shiny leaves.*

run wild over shrubs or hedges. Blackbirds and thrushes will nest among them and will particularly enjoy their fruits and seeds in the autumn.

Bountiful ivy

Many gardeners ruthlessly remove ivy in the belief that it is a tree-killing parasite. It can weaken trees by competing with them for water, minerals and light, and its dense evergreen foliage can severely damage a hedgerow, but it is not a true parasite. Keep it under control by regular trimming and you will find that its benefits far outweigh any disadvantages, as it can feed and shelter a wonderful array of wildlife. Robins, flycatchers, dunnocks and many other birds nest and roost in the foliage; the flowers yield abundant nectar for butterflies and other insects preparing for hibernation in the autumn (see page 102); and the fruits can be life-savers for thrushes and other birds searching for food in the spring.

foliage provides plenty of cover for birds during the summer and it is well worth installing a few nest boxes among the branches. Climbing hydrangea, which flourishes on shady walls, will also offer plenty of shelter to your garden birds. Let honeysuckle, wild roses, brambles and the various forms of *Clematis montana*

RIGHT: *In addition to providing food and safe nesting sites for the birds, fragrant honeysuckle will scent your whole garden on summer evenings.*

ABOVE: *Ivy berries are among the few fruits that ripen in the spring.*

You can grow ivy on walls as well as trees and, if you tie it in to start with, it will even disguise ugly chainlink fences. If you are worried about ivy climbing your walls or trees, buy a bushy non-climbing variety which is just as good for wildlife.

Herbaceous dinner tables

Sunflowers are among my favourite flowers. Their sunny faces, which are often covered with bees and other insects, are almost as good as the sunshine itself, and the pleasure continues even when the flowers have faded, as greenfinches and goldfinches flock to feast on the nodding seed heads. Greenfinches are especially amusing to watch as they use their bills like can-openers to rip open the seeds. If the birds allow any of the seeds to ripen, you can then collect them and use them on your bird table during the winter. Teasels, cultivated thistles, poppies, cornflowers and love-in-a-mist are all very attractive to goldfinches, which sway precariously on the stems while digging out the seeds – often long before they are ripe. And you could do worse than cultivate a patch of dandelions and leave some grass to seed for these birds.

LEFT: *The tubular central florets of the sunflower are full of scent and nectar. When the bees have done their work each flowerhead contains hundreds of nutritious seeds.*

Familiar garden birds

Asked to list their favourite garden birds, most people would put the robin, often known as the 'gardener's friend', at or near the top. Other common visitors to our gardens include the tits and sparrows and a host of finches.

Robins

The robin's song, boldness and cheery appearance have long endeared it to us, and, indeed, it is usually regarded as Britain's national bird.

A recent survey conducted by the British Trust for Ornithology revealed that robins were present in 99 per cent of the gardens surveyed. They stay with us throughout the year, although we do not see or hear much of them for a few weeks during late summer. This is the moulting period, when their old feathers are replaced and flying is curtailed, but as soon as they have regained their red breasts, the birds waste no time in redefining their territories and defending them with song and aggressive displays.

Courtship and nesting

Males and females sing and display with equal vigour, and for several months each bird remains fiercely independent, even attacking any other robin that dares to encroach upon its territory. As autumn turns into winter, however, the barriers begin to come down and the females are allowed into the males' territories.

'Engaged' pairs may feed close to each other, but otherwise have little contact until the spring. The male continues to

RIGHT: *The nestling with the widest gape – usually the hungriest one – will generally get the grub. This is nature's way of ensuring that all the nestlings get their share.*

ABOVE: *A robin will learn to take mealworms from your hand in just a few days. Offer the worms on the ground in front of you at first.*

While the female is building the nest and incubating the eggs, the male feeds her regularly. She utters a short, sharp call to tell him where she is and he obediently shoves some food into her open beak. This courtship feeding is easy to watch once you have located the female. If you maintain a regular feeding station, the male will return to it every few minutes throughout the day, periodically stopping to re-fuel himself between visits to his mate.

defend his territory with song, but the female gradually stops singing and gets ready for the breeding season. She builds the nest unaided in the spring, choosing a fairly low, dark hole if possible.

An open-fronted box, hidden in a dense hedge or on an ivy-clad wall, makes an ideal home. Robins are also said to be happy with an old kettle wedged in a hedge with the spout pointing down to prevent water-logging. However, the one that I placed in my hedge has been totally ignored for 25 years!

Leaves and moss form the bulk of the cup-shaped nest, which is then lined with fine roots and hair. There is usually no shortage of nesting materials in a normal garden, but if you hang up a bag of moss, wool and hair (see page 82) you will be able to enjoy watching the hen tugging out the pieces and cleverly manipulating them with her beak before flying back to her nest. Breeding usually starts in March or April and the robins may raise two or even three broods during the next three or four months.

The menu

Robins will eat almost anything that they can get their slender beaks round or into. Sultanas and other dried fruit, grated cheese, cake crumbs and bird pudding (see page 63) are all very acceptable, but the birds are essentially insect-eaters and they will do almost anything for a feed of mealworms. Once a bird has learned where mealworms are on offer, it will tap on the window to ask for them and may even enter the house to seek them out!

LEFT: *An open-fronted nest box is ideal for robins, especially if it is partly concealed by creepers and other vegetation. Notice that the young robins do not have red breasts. The colour does not develop until the birds moult in late summer.*

Blue tits

Easily identified by the bright blue crown, blue tits are present in virtually every British garden, especially in the winter. You may think there are just a few resident birds in your garden at this bleak time of year, but it is quite likely that dozens of blue tits pass through each day, staying just long enough for a snack.

Blue tits are essentially insectivorous birds, using their tiny pointed beaks to pluck caterpillars, aphids and many other insects from trees in summer. In winter, they scour tree trunks and branches for aphid eggs and spiders, although seeds are more important at this time.

Like all the other tits, the blue tit is an inquisitive bird and readily finds and adapts to new sources of food. The birds display amazing agility while taking peanuts from a variety of feeders, and their habit of pecking through milk bottle tops to get at the cream is equally well known.

Blue tits are hole nesters and, like great tits, they will readily nest in traditional tit-boxes (see page 81). The female builds the nest herself, using plenty of moss and hair or wool, and she alone incubates the eggs while the male bird works hard to keep her supplied with a diet of juicy caterpillars.

BELOW: *The blue tit is a sharp-eyed hunter, able to spot the tiniest of insect eggs in bark crevices and pluck them out with its tweezer-like beak. Give them a comfortable nest box and a pair might well rear a brood of nine or ten babies.*

ABOVE: *The great tit is distinguished from the blue tit by its larger size and black crown.*

ABOVE: *The coal tit has a black crown with a white patch at the rear. It usually feeds high up in the trees, especially in conifers, but comes to bird tables in the winter.*

House sparrows

If you live in a town you might think the house sparrow is one of our commonest birds, but this is far from the truth. House sparrows, distinguished by the dull grey crown, are rarely seen far from human habitation, and huge tracts of the countryside have no house sparrows at all.

House sparrows are very sociable birds and where they occur they are often seen in large numbers, feeding on seeds and any scraps that they can glean from streets and gardens. Although they are basically ground-feeding and not as acrobatic as the tits, they are perfectly happy on the bird table and quite good at extracting peanuts from various feeders.

They usually nest in small colonies, with several pairs of birds living on a few neighbouring properties. The rest of the street may have no nests at all, although the sparrows may well feed there. The untidy nests are made largely of grass and straw but also include wool, feathers and anything that takes the birds' fancy. Give them some cotton wool and watch the fun as they squabble over it! Nests are usually built on houses, especially on creeper-clad walls, or in dense hedges, and the birds appreciate open-fronted boxes or tunnels (see page 84) fixed in sheltered spots. A colony may exist for several years but then, for no obvious reason, leave and settle in another part of the town or village.

ABOVE: *The black bib of the male house sparrow is smaller in winter. Females have no bib at all.*

DECLINING POPULATIONS

House sparrow populations have declined sharply in recent years, the most likely explanation being that modern or modernized houses do not provide enough nesting sites. Whatever the reason for their decline, feeding these sparrows in our gardens can only do good. They might damage a few crocuses and spring flowers as they drink the nectar, but our gardens would be much poorer without these cheerful squabblers.

FAR LEFT: *Although often called a hedge sparrow, the dunnock is not a sparrow at all – look at its much narrower beak. A common garden bird, it nearly always feeds on the ground.*

LEFT: *The tree sparrow differs from the house sparrow in having a chestnut crown and white cheeks with a black patch in the middle.*

Identifying garden birds

Apart from the wren, the birds pictured on these two pages are all finches. Their stout bills indicate that they are essentially seed-eaters, although they are not averse to insects and spiders. Most of them feed their young with insects. The wren's slender, pointed bill shows that it feeds mainly on small insects as it cannot crack hard seeds, but it can deal with most other foods.

▲ Bullfinch (male)

Identification: Male easily identified by black cap and rosy underparts. Look for the white rump in flight. Female similar but duller.
Distribution: Resident everywhere.
Feeding habits: Buds, often removed from our fruit trees and bushes at a rate of 30 buds per minute, form up to 30 per cent of its diet in the spring. Soft fruit is attacked later in the year, so the bird is not usually welcome in the garden.
Nest: Usually low in a thick hedge or bush.
Notes: Birds mate for life; usually seen in pairs.

▲ Siskin (male)

Identification: Yellow rump and tail flashes are conspicuous in flight. Female lacks the male's black cap and bib and is streaky grey below.
Distribution: Resident in many wooded areas, but mainly a winter visitor to gardens.
Feeding habits: Particularly fond of the seeds of conifers and alders but readily takes peanuts from the bird table.
Nest: Usually high in coniferous trees.
Notes: Becoming increasingly common in British gardens in winter.

▶ Serin (female)

Identification: Look for the tiny beak and the bright yellow rump in flight. Male has bright yellow head and breast. Female is duller, with brown streaks on the breast.
Distribution: A common town and garden bird in southern Europe, but a scarce summer visitor to the British Isles, mainly in the south.
Feeding habits: Feeds mainly on the ground.
Nest: In thick conifers or in citrus groves.
Notes: A rather restless bird.

▲ Chaffinch (male)

Identification: Look for the broad white shoulder flash and wing bar. The male's slate-blue head and rust-red face are very distinctive in summer but less bright in winter. The female is much browner.
Distribution: Resident everywhere.
Feeding habits: A regular visitor to garden feeding stations, but more often seen scouring the ground below than perching on the table.
Nest: A neat cup of moss and lichen wedged into the fork of a tree or shrub.
Notes: One of Britain's commonest birds.

▲ Greenfinch (male)

Identification: Look for the narrow yellow edge to the wing. Male has a greyish-green back, but female has a brown tinge and dark streaks. Both sexes show yellow tail flashes in flight.
Distribution: Resident almost everywhere.
Feeding habits: Takes seeds from trees and many herbaceous plants, including sunflowers, and is very partial to peanuts. Also eats buds.
Nest: A bulky cup wedged in the fork of a tree or tall shrub, usually some kind of conifer.
Notes: Often forms small flocks in winter.

▲ Goldfinch

Identification: Look for the red face and golden wing bars. The sexes are alike.
Distribution: Resident almost everywhere.
Feeding habits: Feeds mainly on the seeds of herbaceous plants, often balancing acrobatically on the flower-heads to pull out the seeds before they are ripe. The bird will also take crushed seeds from the bird table.
Nest: A neat cup built in a tree or tall shrub.
Notes: Most common in gardens in late summer and autumn, when the birds may form flocks.

▲ Wren

Identification: Plump and rounded, with tail often distinctively cocked. Look for the prominent eye-stripe and the dark bars on the wings and tail. The sexes are alike.
Distribution: Resident almost everywhere.
Feeding habits: Eats insects and spiders and also takes crumbs from under the bird table.
Nest: A ball of moss and leaves, usually built in some kind of hole: sometimes nests in tit-boxes.
Notes: Britain's commonest bird, although not the commonest garden bird. Often mistaken for a mouse as its scuttles through the undergrowth.

▲ Collared dove

Identification: Look for the conspicuous black collar on the delicate pinkish-grey plumage. The sexes are alike.

Distribution: Resident almost everywhere.

Feeding habits: Basically a grain-eater, the collared dove enjoys virtually all the vegetable foods that we offer, but rarely feeds other than on the ground.

Nest: A flimsy platform of twigs, usually in a tree but sometimes on a building.

Notes: Almost unknown in Europe 100 years ago, the collared dove now occurs almost all over the continent and its monotonous *coo-cooo-cu* can be heard in nearly every garden.

▲ Jackdaw

Identification: The grey neck distinguishes this bird from other members of the crow family. The sexes are alike.

Distribution: Resident almost everywhere.

Feeding habits: Omnivorous, often seen tugging worms and insect grubs from lawns. It may kill and eat the nestlings of other birds, and also eats a lot of fruit, especially cherries.

Nest: An untidy accumulation of twigs, lined with wool and assorted plant fibres and usually built in a hole. Chimneys are often used, as are large open-fronted nest boxes.

Notes: The birds mate for life and are usually seen in pairs.

◀ Starling

Identification: Essentially black with strong purple and green iridescence and pale spots. The latter are most obvious in winter and gradually disappear in spring as the tips of the feathers wear away. The rather long bill of the starling is yellow in summer and brown in winter. The young birds are dull brown. Starlings strut over the ground and do not hop in the way that most other garden birds do. The sexes are alike.

Distribution: Resident almost everywhere.

Feeding habits: Omnivorous, taking anything that is offered on the bird table: very fond of fallen apples in autumn. It is often regarded as a 'bully' because it commonly chases smaller birds away.

Nest: Usually in a hole in a wall or a tree, but also in well-concealed open-fronted nest boxes.

Notes: Forms huge roosting flocks in winter.

▲ Pied wagtail (male)

Identification: Look for the long tail, the white forehead, and the black crown. Female is greyer. Throat of both sexes becomes white in winter.
Distribution: Resident in much of Western Europe: summer visitor in north and east.
Feeding habits: Insectivorous and most often seen snapping up insects on lawns or by ponds. Takes crumbs from the bird table in winter.
Nest: In holes, often in dry stone walls: may use open-fronted boxes if these are well concealed.
Notes: One of the few insectivorous species to stay with us through the winter, the bird is named for the vigorous wagging of its long tail.

▲ House martin

Identification: Look for the black back, white rump, pure white underparts, and short, forked tail. The sexes are alike.
Distribution: Summer visitor to all of Europe, but most common around human habitation.
Feeding habits: Insectivorous and most often seen catching flies and other small insects in full flight high above the garden.
Nest: A mud cup fixed to cliffs and walls, under the eaves of buildings. The birds may also use boxes of the appropriate shape (see page 84).
Notes: Providing mud and feathers may encourage the birds to nest on your house.

▲ Spotted flycatcher

Identification: Greyish-brown back and dirty white underparts which are streaked with brown. The sexes are alike.
Distribution: Summer visitor to all of Europe.
Feeding habits: Catches a variety of insects by darting out from a perch and snapping them up in mid-air. It usually returns to its perch to eat.
Nest: In holes or on ledges; readily uses open-fronted boxes.
Notes: May be confused with the dunnock (see page 73), but latter is browner and has red legs.

▲ Swallow

Identification: Look for the red face and throat and the long forked tail. The sexes are alike.
Distribution: Summer visitor to all of Europe; most common around farms and villages.
Feeding habits: Insectivorous, catching small insects in mid air, although usually flying at lower levels and often just above the ground.
Nest: A cup of mud and feathers, usually built on a ledge in or on a building.
Notes: Often drinks while skimming over the water surface.

▲ Blackbird (male)

Identification: Male is glossy black with a yellow bill. Female is dark brown with faint spotting on the breast and a brown bill.
Distribution: Resident in most parts of Europe, but only a summer visitor in the north.
Feeding habits: Omnivorous, but especially fond of earthworms and fruit: a regular visitor at, or more often under, the bird table.
Nest: In shrubs, hedgerows and creepers; made largely with grass and mud.
Notes: One of Britain's commonest birds.

▲ Fieldfare

Identification: Look for the grey head and the heavily streaked buff breast. The pale grey rump is very conspicuous in flight. The sexes are alike.
Distribution: Breeds in northern and central Europe, but a winter visitor to most other parts.
Feeding habits: Scours gardens and hedgerows for fruit in winter and may come to the bird table. Worms and insects are eaten in summer.
Nest: A bulky cup of mud and grass, built anywhere from the ground to the tree tops.
Notes: Forms large flocks in cold winters.

▲ Song thrush

Identification: Look for the plain brown back and the buff and white underparts heavily marked with more or less triangular black spots.
Distribution: Resident in most of western Europe, but only a summer visitor in the north.
Feeding habits: Omnivorous, taking lots of fruit and earthworms as well as finding plenty of interest on the bird table. But snails are a favourite food and the birds can often be heard smashing the shells against stones.
Nest: Built with grass and mud in shrubs, hedges and creepers.
Notes: Mistle thrush is greyer with more rounded spots.

▲ Blackcap (female)

Identification: Male has a sooty black crown; female crown is rust-red. The other plumage is brown or grey, with no black on the throat.
Distribution: Resident in south-west Europe, including southern Britain and Ireland; a summer visitor elsewhere.
Feeding habits: Insects and spiders are main foods in spring and summer, but fruits and seeds dominate in autumn, with elderberries being a great favourite.
Nest: Low down in thick shrubs and hedgerows.
Notes: Once only a summer visitor to the British Isles, it is now resident in some places and we also get winter visitors from central Europe.

▲ Green woodpecker

Identification: The red crown and green back are unmistakable. The sexes are alike.

Distribution: Resident in most wooded parts of Europe except Ireland and the far north.

Feeding habits: The green woodpecker sometimes digs insects from tree trunks, but is usually seen quartering the lawn in search of its favourite food – ants.

Nest: A hole excavated in a tree trunk.

Notes: Its loud, chuckling call has given the bird its alternative name of yaffle.

▲ Great spotted woodpecker

Identification: Look for the deep red patch under the tail and the large white wing patch. Only the male has a red spot at the back of the head.

Distribution: Resident in wooded areas almost all over Europe but not in Ireland.

Feeding habits: Digs insects from tree trunks and eats nuts and seeds. Delights in removing peanuts you care to wedge into bark crevices.

Nest: A hole excavated in a tree trunk; will use tit boxes after enlarging the opening.

Notes: Lesser spotted woodpecker is much smaller; male has a red crown but there is never any red underneath.

▶ Nuthatch

Identification: Blue-grey crown and back, rusty brown underparts and black eye-stripe. The sexes are alike.

Distribution: Resident in most of Europe, but not Ireland or northern Britain.

Feeding habits: Digs insects and spiders from bark crevices and wedges in hazel nuts before hammering them open with its sturdy beak.

Nest: In tree holes, but readily accepts tit boxes.

Notes: The only bird that can run down a tree trunk as easily as it can climb up.

Houses for birds

Feeding the birds in your garden can provide them with a vital lifeline in the winter and can give you a great deal of fun as well, so why not go a step further and actually give the birds somewhere to live?

You can then enjoy watching the parents building their nests and feeding the young, and later you will be able to watch the young birds learning to fly. Many birds readily take to nest boxes, especially if natural sites are in short supply – as they often are in small and new gardens.

Making a nest box

This is actually very easy – you don't even have to be good at carpentry, just able to saw fairly straight and glue, screw or nail a few pieces of wood together. The birds will probably appreciate the ventilation

RIGHT: *Decide where you are going to site your tit box before you make the entrance hole, and then make sure that it is on the right side: where you can see it but away from the prevailing wind. The latch is not essential, but it does prevent the lid from lifting in a strong wind.*

produced by a few gaps. The two basic types of nest box – the traditional tit box, beloved by blue tits and great tits and also by wrens and nuthatches, and the open-fronted box, favoured by robins and flycatchers, can both be made from a single plank of wood, as shown in the diagrams opposite.

However, if this does not appeal to you, it is possible to buy a wide range of 'designer' boxes from pet shops and other suppliers (see page 83). Don't be tempted by fancy, colourful boxes. They might look attractive to you, but the birds prefer natural materials and colours. Avoid plastic boxes also as they will overheat and sweat in the summer.

When and where

Don't wait until the nesting season to put up your boxes; get them into position well before Christmas so that the birds have plenty of time to get used to them. Wrens, tits and other small birds may well roost in the boxes on cold winter nights.

◆ **Tit boxes** can be fixed to walls and tree trunks, sheltered from the full sun so that the eggs and babies won't be cooked. Make sure that the boxes are firmly fixed and cannot sway in the wind.

◆ **Open-fronted boxes** always need to be concealed among climbing plants on a

MAKING A TIT BOX

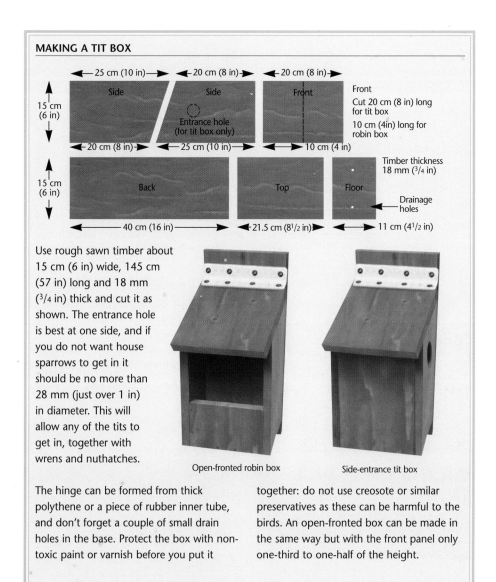

25 cm (10 in)   20 cm (8 in)   20 cm (8 in)

15 cm (6 in)

Side   Side   Front   Front

Entrance hole (for tit box only)

Cut 20 cm (8 in) long for tit box

10 cm (4in) long for robin box

20 cm (8 in)   25 cm (10 in)   10 cm (4 in)

15 cm (6 in)

Back   Top   Floor

Timber thickness 18 mm ($^3/_4$ in)

Drainage holes

40 cm (16 in)   21.5 cm (8$^1/_2$ in)   11 cm (4$^1/_2$ in)

Use rough sawn timber about 15 cm (6 in) wide, 145 cm (57 in) long and 18 mm ($^3/_4$ in) thick and cut it as shown. The entrance hole is best at one side, and if you do not want house sparrows to get in it should be no more than 28 mm (just over 1 in) in diameter. This will allow any of the tits to get in, together with wrens and nuthatches.

Open-fronted robin box   Side-entrance tit box

The hinge can be formed from thick polythene or a piece of rubber inner tube, and don't forget a couple of small drain holes in the base. Protect the box with non-toxic paint or varnish before you put it together: do not use creosote or similar preservatives as these can be harmful to the birds. An open-fronted box can be made in the same way but with the front panel only one-third to one-half of the height.

LEAVE THE BIRDS ALONE

It is very tempting to lift the lid and take a peep at the eggs or babies, but don't do it. You could cause the parent birds to abandon the nest and leave their eggs or babies to die. And remember: disturbing nesting birds is against the law.

wall or a pergola, or otherwise securely fixed in a hedge.

◆ **All boxes** must be high enough to be out of reach of cats, preferably more than 2 m (6 ft) above the ground.

You might like to fix some kind of landing platform close to the box. The birds will not always use it, but if they do you will get a better view of what food and nesting materials they bring in. You will also have a much better chance of photographing your guests.

Apart from house sparrows and house martins, most of our garden birds are territorial and they spread their nests out so that they can all get enough food for their young. So, although several different kinds of birds may use your nest boxes, don't expect more than one pair of each species to nest in a small garden.

You can clean out your nest boxes in the autumn, but make sure that the birds have finished with them before you start. Rubber gloves will protect you from the many fleas that will undoubtedly remain in the boxes. Scrub the boxes with soapy water and give the outside another coat of non-toxic paint if necessary.

Nesting materials

Hang up net bags stuffed with building materials at the beginning of the nesting season and watch the birds collect what they need. The easier it is for them to collect nesting material, the more likely they are to nest in your garden – and the more energy they will have to rear their families. Wool, string, feathers and straw are all suitable, and it is worth adding a handful of hair, easily obtained from your hairdresser's floor. Avoid brightly coloured materials, which might make a nest more conspicuous to predators.

ABOVE: *Large open-fronted nest boxes, about 30 cm (12 in) high and having a floor area of about 50 cm² (20 in²), may attract kestrels if they are placed high in a tree.*

ABOVE: *Open-fronted nest boxes require more shelter than tit boxes. Place them among creepers on a wall or tree trunk or fix them under the eaves of your house. This one is being used by spotted flycatchers.*

RIGHT: *Tree creepers may be confused with sparrows but they are readily distinguished by their curved beak and white underside. They normally nest behind loose bark, so this narrow box fixed to a tree trunk provides them with an ideal home.*

LEFT: *This tit box has an anti-predator device. Cats, squirrels and other predators are amazingly clever at reaching nest boxes that you think are out of their reach, and they kill lots of nestling birds. This simple device fitted around the entrance hole prevents the predators from reaching into the box and getting at the nestlings.*

ABOVE: *The apex nest box is a variation on the traditional tit box; this one is being used by a family of blue tits. The surrounding creepers give the birds somewhere to perch before diving into the box, but they are even more useful for the babies when they first leave the nest. If you are lucky you could see half a dozen or more lining up on the branches ready for their first flying lessons.*

LEFT: *Made from a mixture of wood and cement, Schwegler boxes come in a wide range of designs, suitable for all kinds of birds. Tough and long-lasting, they also have remarkable insulating properties that cut down temperature fluctuation inside and reduce the problem of condensation.*

LEFT: *The natural look: you can make a tit box from a log about 25 cm (10 in) long and 15 cm (6 in) in diameter. Silver birch makes a very attractive box, but any wood will do. Cut a slice off each end and then slice the log lengthways through the centre. Hollow out each half with a saw, then glue them back together. Drill an entrance hole on one side and glue or screw the two ends back on to complete the box.*

Specialist boxes

House martins may fix their mud cups tight up under the eaves of your house if there is a handy supply of mud, and you can encourage them by using artificial nests made from papier-maché. Even if the martins do not move into this ready-made accommodation, they may build close to it, and once you have one or more nests, the birds will probably return to them year after year. A bowl of nice sticky mud can be a further inducement to nesting, especially if there are no convenient natural supplies. House martin colonies do make a mess with their droppings, but you can overcome this by placing a shelf under the nests and periodically scraping off the 'guano'.

Tunnel boxes fixed under the eaves are ideal for house sparrows, and may also attract spotted flycatchers. Little more than elongated, open-fronted boxes, the tunnels can be made with just two short planks screwed or glued together and fixed into a corner so that there is just one opening. Larger tunnels, closed at one end and securely fixed in large trees, may attract tawny owls, and if you can fix an old tea chest high in a barn you can reasonably look forward to playing host to a family of barn owls. In many parts of the continent, it is worth putting up a platform for the white storks, whose huge nests of sticks and straw often have sparrows squatting in the lower levels.

ABOVE: *Strapped to the underside of a large branch, a wooden tube, 75 x 20 cm (30 x 8 in) may attract a pair of tawny owls.*

ABOVE: *These white storks have built their untidy nest on a specially erected platform on a house. The birds usually return to the same site each year, adding fresh material each time, so old nests reach enormous proportions.*

RIGHT: *House martin boxes are easily screwed under the eaves of the house. However, they are often taken over by house sparrows.*

Dealing with casualties

Injured birds are notoriously difficult to treat and it is usually kinder to put badly injured birds out of their misery. However, if there is no obvious sign of injury, a bit of tender care can restore the birds to fitness.

The most frequent garden casualty is the bird that flies into a window pane and knocks itself out. Such accidents are associated particularly with large picture windows, especially when there is a window on each side of a room and the bird thinks it can fly right through. Although the crash can create plenty of noise and scatter a lot of feathers, the birds are not usually badly hurt and they can normally be nursed back to health in a short time. It is certainly better to try this than to leave the birds on the ground for a passing predatory cat.

Put the casualty in a shoe box or similar container with some soft bedding. Put the lid on, and keep it in a quiet place until you hear the bird moving. If you then take it outside it will probably fly away. You can even nurse the bird on your lap if you have no suitable box. Half an hour's rest is often enough for the bird to make a full recovery.

Reluctance to fly may indicate a damaged wing, but the bird may still recover. Put it in a cage for a few days and feed it with mealworms or with a seed mixture designed for wild birds. If it is still no better, you can try taking it to your local vet, but the bird will probably have to be destroyed.

Prevention is always better than cure and you can greatly reduce the risk of

ABOVE: *Its first excursion cut short by a collision with a window, this young blackbird quickly recovered with a bit of warmth.*

collisions by sticking cut-outs of hawks on large windows. This will keep the small birds away from the windows.

Baby birds

Fledglings leaving their nests for the first time often fall to the ground and look lost. It is tempting to give them a hand, but the kindest thing is to leave them alone because their parents are probably gathering food for them nearby. If you keep your cat indoors, the young birds will be relatively safe in your garden, and the parent birds will probably return to help their babies to safety and encourage them to fly.

PART FOUR

Reptiles and Amphibians

Unlike mammals and birds, reptiles and amphibians are cold-blooded animals, but this does not mean that they are always cold. Their body temperatures vary with those of the surrounding air or water, so the animals can actually be quite warm.

Amphibians are represented in the garden by frogs, toads and newts. Gardens in southern Europe may harbour the beautiful green tree frog (left) and may also be home to the fire salamander. All have thin, mucus-covered skin and all are confined to damp places. Apart from the fire salamander, our garden species all pass through an aquatic tadpole stage as they grow up. All are carnivorous, feeding on worms, slugs and a wide range of other invertebrates. They sleep through the winter in compost heaps and log-piles, or in the mud at the bottom of ponds.

Reptiles are represented in the garden mainly by lizards and snakes. The animals are covered with scales and, contrary to popular opinion, they are never slimy. Most of them prefer drier and warmer places than the amphibians and they need to warm up by basking in the morning sunshine before they can get going. They are most common in the south, and in all but the warmest areas, the reptiles sleep through the winter.

Lizards

Three species of lizards are native to the British mainland, but only the common or viviparous lizard and the slow worm are likely to occur in gardens. Both are carnivorous, eating a wide range of insects, spiders and other invertebrates.

FEEDING LIZARDS

Most lizards can be tempted with some mealworms (see page 64). If you have lizards in the garden, put out a saucer of mealworms and sit back and watch the fun. As long as you keep still, you can stay quite close – and then the birds won't pinch all the worms.

The viviparous lizard is a sun-loving creature and a good way of attracting it to your garden is to leave areas of short grass or bare ground or, better still, a few rocks on which it can sunbathe. Basking is especially important for this lizard because the females give birth to active young and they need warmth for the proper development of the babies. Most other lizards lay eggs. Dry stone walls and log piles are also good places for the lizards, as long as they get some sunshine. They provide warm surfaces for basking, and their numerous nooks and crannies are ideal sleeping and breeding quarters. And, of course, they harbour plenty of tasty small animals.

The legless lizard

The slow worm is often mistaken for a small snake, but this legless lizard is fairly easy to recognize by its rather uniform shiny brown colour. Its oval eye, equipped with eyelids, is also very different from the circular eyes of snakes. Not keen on sunshine, the slow worm is most likely to be seen in the evening or after a shower, for this is when the slugs are most active and the slow worm loves slugs! It hunts in hedge bottoms and in long grass at the bases of walls and trees, so try to leave patches of grass for this helpful guest. You may also find it in the compost heap, where it enjoys warmth as well as plenty of slugs.

RIGHT: *Early morning is a good time to lift slow worm shelters. This is often an ideal opportunity to get a good look at the animals when they are still quite cool and lethargic.*

LEFT: *The green lizard, seen here in a typical basking pose, is easily recognized by its colour. Adults are a much brighter green than the immature individual shown here.*

You can encourage slow worms to take up residence in a rough part of the garden by laying down a few pieces of old carpet or some curved roof tiles. These objects make ideal shelters for slow worms because the animals can get comfortably warm without actually exposing themselves to the sun. Lift the shelters occasionally to see the animals; unlike snakes and other lizards, they tend to sit tight when disturbed and are easy to examine. Slow worms give birth to active young and you may find the babies – like shiny pieces of string – under the shelters in the autumn.

Continental lizards

Continental gardens and those in the Channel Islands also support green and wall lizards. With a body about 12 cm (5 in) long and a tail up to twice as much again, the green lizard is one of our largest species. Each individual defends a territory, often a large clump of grass or other dense vegetation on which it can bask, but the lizards are very touchy and all you usually see is a tail disappearing

into the undergrowth. Wall lizards are much easier to watch. Living in and around our houses, they bask on any sunny surface and scamper up and down walls with amazing agility. Give them some old tiles to bask on and, as long as you don't move too quickly, you will be able to watch them quite easily.

LEFT: *The common or viviparous lizard, seen here basking on a sunny log, has a relatively smaller head than the wall lizard pictured below.*

LEFT: *True to its name, the wall lizard is a great climber, running up and down walls with equal ease and snapping up any spider or insect coming within its range.*

Snakes

Snakes probably like gardeners even less than gardeners like snakes, and they are likely to take up residence only in the wilder and less tidy gardens where they are subjected to minimal disturbance. Unless we are extremely quiet, they usually slither away before we even notice them.

Britain has just three native snake species, and only two of these are at all likely to be found in our gardens: the adder, which is poisonous, and the grass snake, which is not. In Scotland, only the adder occurs and, thanks to St Patrick, there are no snakes at all in Ireland.

Snakes in the grass

The grass snake, also known as the ringed snake because of its conspicuous yellow collar, is Britain's biggest snake. It can be as much as 2 m (6 ft) long, although it is usually a good deal shorter. It likes damp grassy places and feeds mainly on frogs and toads. Some small birds and mammals are also eaten. There is not a lot that you can do to attract this or, indeed, any other snake into your garden and, although there is no reason to fear this harmless creature, not many people are likely to want to encourage it. If you have a meadow or other area of long grass that is cut from time to time, pile the debris in a sunny spot and you may find a grass snake basking there. It might even lay its eggs in the heap, taking advantage of the warmth generated by the rotting grass. The grass snake is also attracted to compost heaps, which provide it with food as well as warmth.

Beware of the zig-zag

Adders occur in all kinds of rough habitats. They are rare in gardens, where they are most likely to be found in sunny spots at

RIGHT: *The grass snake's forked tongue is not a weapon. As in all snakes, it is simply used to pick up scent. When scared, the snake may fool its enemies by pretending to be dead.*

the bases of hedges and old walls. Look for the dark zig-zag line on this snake's back. Adders feed mainly on small mammals, which are poisoned by its venom. The snakes are rarely dangerous to healthy people, apart from the elderly and the very young, but if you do have adders in the area and you don't particularly want to watch them it is worth stamping your feet every few yards as you walk around – the vibration will send the snakes slithering for cover. Never jump across ditches or other obstacles: you might just land on a basking adder. I have done it myself and was lucky not to be bitten!

ABOVE: *Rarely more than 65 cm (26 in) long, the adder ranges from pale grey to chestnut, but the zig-zag pattern is usually quite distinct.*

Southern snakes

Gardens in Italy and the southern half of France often harbour the western whip snake, but don't expect to see much more than the tail end disappearing silently into the vegetation or under a wall, as this is one of the fastest snakes. It enjoys sunbathing, and if you suspect it may be in the vicinity, it is worth putting down a couple of paving slabs or creating a patch of close-mown turf in an area of longer grass. Set up your sun-bed or deckchair nearby and you may be able to watch this handsome snake. It is non-poisonous and feeds largely on lizards.

LEFT: *Usually identified by its bold black and yellow pattern, the western whip snake is a good climber, although it is most likely to be seen on the ground.*

Frogs, toads and newts

All these animals are amphibians and, true to their name, they spend part of their life in water and part on land. However, even on land they have to stay in damp places because their thin skins are not waterproof. In fact, they suffocate if they get dry.

CONSERVATION TIP

Do not import any frogspawn into your pond from another area as you might unwittingly introduce red-leg virus, which can kill frogs. Get some spawn from a neighbour's pond which you know is free from the disease.

RIGHT: *The smooth skin and the dark patch behind the eye distinguish the common frog – the only one likely to be found in British gardens – from the common toad below.*

RIGHT: *The typically warty skin of the toads is clearly evident in this common toad. Despite their long back legs, toads tend to crawl rather than leap.*

Frogs and toads always live on land in the summer. They are active mainly at night and find their way into many gardens. Frogs eat lots of slugs and small snails, together with worms, woodlice and a wide variety of insects. Toads tend to eat fewer slugs but more woodlice and insects, especially ants. Because the animals have to return to the water to breed, installing

a pond is the best way to encourage them to stay around your garden. Unfortunately, the loss of so many farm and village ponds during the twentieth century meant that the animals became scarce in many areas. Luckily, this decline has been reversed in the last few years by the growing popularity of garden ponds.

Frogs and newts may colonize your pond as soon as it is installed and breed there in its first spring, but toads are extraordinarily faithful to the ponds in which they grew up and are more likely to struggle across a kilometre of countryside to get back home rather than settle down in a new pond. Therefore the best way to establish a toad population is to scrounge some spawn or tadpoles from a neighbouring pond with a good population.

Sleeping through the winter

Short days and falling temperatures in autumn stimulate our amphibians to find safe hideaways where they can sleep through the winter. Most of them burrow into the ground or leaf litter, but log piles and compost heaps are equally acceptable. Clusters of frogs, toads and newts may all pile into the same safe shelter. Newts and

ABOVE: *The blood vessels of this female common newt are clearly visible through the thin skin around the mouth. Because their lungs are not very efficient, amphibians get much of their oxygen through their skins. The oxygen dissolves in the moisture on the skin and then passes into tiny blood vessels which are just below the surface.*

frogs may also sleep at the bottom of a pond: being dormant, they can get enough oxygen from the water as long as there are not too many dead leaves around them. Rotting leaves use up a lot of oxygen, so remove most of the debris from the bottom of your pond in the autumn. Don't leave it until the winter or you will disturb and possibly kill the sleeping animals.

Balletic newts

Newts lack voices and, instead of grabbing the first female to come along, the male courts the female with an elegant dance, fluttering his fine crest and frilly tail, both of which enlarge at the start of the breeding season. The dancing may last for hours and is easy to watch in a garden pond. There is no mating: once the male feels that his dancing has sufficiently impressed the female, he drops a packet of sperm and she picks it up in her genital opening. Over the following few weeks she lays 200 to 300 eggs, wrapping each one carefully in a leaf. Whereas frogs and toads leave soon after mating, newts may stay in the water for much of the summer, eating worms and other small animals.

CONSERVATION TIP

The great crested or warty newt may turn up in your pond. This largely black newt, up to 15 cm (6 in) long, is strictly protected and you must not disturb it in any way. Just enjoy having one of our rarities as a guest, remembering that it is doing good in your garden even if it does eat some of your frog tadpoles – there are usually far more than your pond can support.

If you have trouble with newts eating your frogspawn and young tadpoles, it is worth lifting out the spawn and putting it back in a net of mesh, fine enough to keep out newts. Although you must release the tadpoles when they start to feed, at least some of them will be able to escape from the newts.

RIGHT: *Once he has gripped his mate in a loving embrace, the male frog is extremely difficult to dislodge. The pair will bask and swim around together until the female has shed her eggs.*

A frog's life

Waking from its winter sleep, a frog will soon turn its attention to the important business of breeding; this is something that you can easily follow in your garden pond. Unless it slept in the mud at the bottom of the pond, the frog's first objective is to find some water and it can travel as far as a kilometre to reach it. Males usually arrive first, sometimes as early as January in the warmer parts of the country, and their noisy choruses, which sound like the distant roar of motorcycles, can be heard for several weeks. The common frog has no external vocal sacs, but several species amplify their calls with balloon-like swellings under or at the sides of the throat.

A tight embrace

A female frog, on entering the water, is immediately grabbed by an amorous male, who locks his front legs tightly across her chest. The pair may stay like this for a week or more, and you will occasionally see two males locked on to a single female. Fertilization takes place in the water, with the male releasing his sperm as up to 2,000 little black eggs stream from the female's body. A layer of jelly around each egg absorbs water and swells up within a few hours to form the familiar mass of spawn. Because all the females in a pond spawn at about the same time, the whole pond may turn into a mass of jelly.

Eggs that avoid being eaten by newts and other animals become comma-shaped in a week or so, depending on temperature, and a few days later the jelly liquefies and the tadpoles wriggle free. About 10 mm ($^1/_3$ in) long, they cling to disintegrating jelly or to neighbouring plants for a while before starting to graze on the algae or to suck up debris rich in micro-organisms from the bottom of the pond. A tadpole has external gills at first, like tiny feathers sprouting from its neck, but these are soon replaced by internal gills like those of fishes (see the diagram opposite).

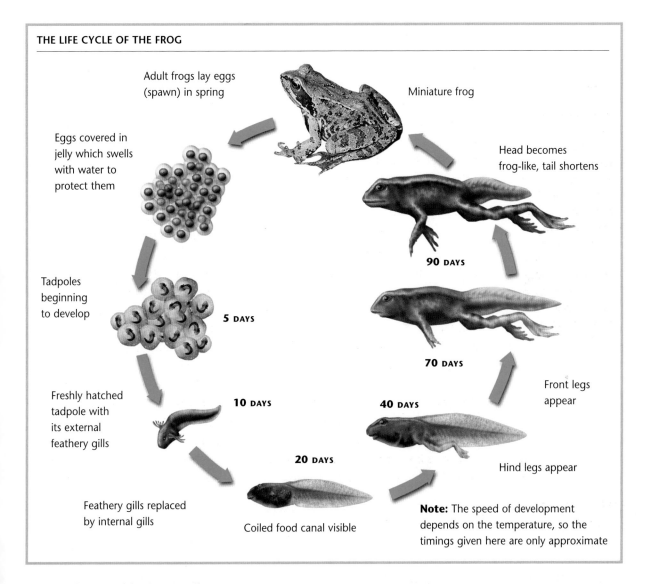

THE LIFE CYCLE OF THE FROG

Adult frogs lay eggs (spawn) in spring

Miniature frog

Eggs covered in jelly which swells with water to protect them

Head becomes frog-like, tail shortens

90 DAYS

Tadpoles beginning to develop

5 DAYS

70 DAYS

Front legs appear

Freshly hatched tadpole with its external feathery gills

10 DAYS

40 DAYS

20 DAYS

Hind legs appear

Feathery gills replaced by internal gills

Coiled food canal visible

Note: The speed of development depends on the temperature, so the timings given here are only approximate

Getting legs and losing a tail

When it is about six weeks old, the tadpole begins its metamorphosis or transformation into a frog. Tiny back legs appear at the base of the tail, soon followed by first the left front leg and then the right one. The body becomes more angular and the eyes become more prominent. The tail is gradually absorbed into the body and grazing on algae gives way to a diet of animal food. No longer a tadpole, the little froglet leaves the water when it is about three months old and hunts for insects and other small animals on land. It will appreciate plenty of plant cover around your pond at this stage. As it grows up, the froglet may move right away from the pond, although always sticking to damp places. If it evades its numerous enemies it will return to the water to start the cycle again when it is about three years old.

PART FIVE

Insects and Other Invertebrates

The invertebrates are the 'creepy-crawlies' of the garden. They are totally lacking in bone and what skeletons they have are on the outside of the body, in the form of a shell or a tough, horny coat. They far outnumber the backboned animals, the vertebrates, and there are literally millions of individuals in your garden, belonging to hundreds or even thousands of different species. It has been estimated that there are 20 million microscopic roundworms to a square metre of soil in some areas, and 90,000 individuals have been found in a single rotting apple.

This teeming assortment of mini-beasts plays a major role in the ecology of the garden, as food for larger creatures and also as re-cycling agents, but only three major groups are likely to be noticed by the gardener. These are the annelids or earthworms, the molluscs (slugs and snails), and the arthropods. The latter are by far the largest of all animal groups, containing insects, spiders, centipedes, millipedes and woodlice. Most of these small animals will find their way into your garden unaided.

Butterflies

Butterflies are the most colourful of all our garden guests and second only to birds in popularity. One of the best things about gardening for butterflies is that these insects appreciate the same sorts of plants as we do, so you can feel free to fill your garden with beds of vibrantly coloured flowers and then sit back and wait for the butterflies to arrive, making it even more colourful.

Although young butterflies (caterpillars) generally need native plants, on which they have been feeding for generations, adult butterflies are happy with a wide range of both exotic and native plants. This is because the sugary nectar on which they feed is much the same in all flowers, but not all cultivated flowers are equally attractive to the insects. Big, showy, double flowers often lack nectar because the nectaries have been replaced by additional petals. The old-fashioned cottage garden flowers, with plenty of scent and nectar, are usually the best of the cultivated forms.

BELOW: *Honesty is doubly useful to the orange tip butterfly: the flowers provide energy-rich nectar whereas the leaves and seed capsules are a source of food for the caterpillars.*

RIGHT: *The ice plant is a superb source of nectar for butterflies seeking an autumn feast before going into hibernation. Here the flowers are playing host to a throng of small tortoiseshell butterflies and a solitary red admiral.*

LEFT: *Corn marigold and Virginia stock contribute both colour and valuable butterfly-attracting nectar to the garden.*

ABOVE: *Polyanthus flowers provide early nectar for brimstones and other butterflies waking from hibernation, and also feed some of the early bees.*

Encouraging butterflies

The 2001 Garden Butterfly Survey, which was organized by Butterfly Conservation, recorded 46 butterfly species in British gardens – just over 70 per cent of the total British species – although the average gardener will be lucky to see more than about 15 or so regular visitors. You can, however, increase the numbers of both species and individuals by growing the right kinds of plants, which should be massed where possible and situated in full sunlight. Different varieties often have different flowering times, and by planting two or more varieties you can increase the period of your garden's attractiveness to butterflies. Regular dead-heading can also prolong the flowering season, but always remember to leave some seeds for the birds.

PLANTS FOR BUTTERFLIES

The following list of butterfly-friendly plants, arranged more or less in chronological order of flowering, will help you to choose a good assortment for your garden, although your soil may not be suitable for all of them.

* Denotes wild flowers native to Britain
** There are several varieties of this popular garden plant, but they are not all particularly good for butterflies. The original pale-flowered form is best. The dark-flowered 'Autumn Joy' looks good, but has little nectar and butterflies are not keen on it.

- Polyanthus
- Aubretia
- Wallflower
- Cuckoo flower*
- Honesty
- Sweet rocket
- Bugle*
- Red valerian*
- Ragged robin*
- Mignonette*
- Sweet William
- Corn marigold*
- Sainfoin*
- Lavender
- Phlox

- Marjoram*
- Common knapweed*
- Field scabious*
- Globe thistle
- Fleabane*
- Hemp agrimony*
- Purple loosestrife*
- Helichrysum
- Golden rod
- Verbena
- Buddleia
- Dahlia (single)
- Michaelmas daisy
- Ice-plant (*Sedum spectabile*)**

ABOVE: *Marjoram is a great favourite with the gatekeeper or hedge brown butterfly.*

Butterfly bushes

So strong is the attraction of buddleia for butterflies that it is commonly called the butterfly bush. Many people plant it purely to bring in the butterflies, although it is an attractive plant in its own right. Buddleia has several species, but the various forms of *B. davidii* are the most butterfly-friendly bushes, and those with pale mauve flowers seem to be the best of all. The darker ones, although very striking to look at, often have little nectar and attract far fewer butterflies. *B. davidii* usually flowers from late June until September, but you can extend the flowering period by tinkering with your pruning regime. Leave one bush more or less unpruned and it will flower somewhat earlier than another which is pruned hard in the normal way in the spring. The globular, orange-yellow flower

clusters of the evergreen *B. globosa* open in May – a month or more before *B. davidii* comes into flower – and these will pull in a varied range of early butterflies.

I have a sneaking admiration for unkempt privet hedges that are left to flower in the summer, for it was on such a hedge that I met my first red admiral and painted lady. Many other butterflies

---

VITAL STINGING NETTLES

If you want butterflies to breed in your garden, you will have to provide the larval food-plants – and for some of our most colourful species, including the peacock and

red admiral, this means planting stinging nettles! Few gardeners are prepared to tolerate these invasive plants, but if you have space, it is worth cultivating a small patch. If the caterpillars don't eat them you can always cook them yourself – not a bad substitute for spinach! Ignore the temptation to relegate your nettle patch to a dark corner; the butterflies will ignore it there as well because they like to lay their eggs in sunshine. Cut the patch regularly, a bit at a time, so that there is always some young growth available for the insects.

And don't be too eager to trim round the bases of trees, walls and hedges; a bit of long grass here may feed the caterpillars of ringlets and gatekeepers.

LEFT: *Map butterfly larvae*

LEFT: *No wildlife garden should be without a buddleia. Even a solitary bush in a town garden will attract butterflies, and it is easy to watch them plunging their long tongues into the nectar-filled tubular flowers. Although it is unlikely to be seen in many British gardens, the swallowtail is a common visitor to continental gardens.*

are attracted by the heady scent and strong nectar. Bramble is another favourite, providing nectar for the gatekeepers and ringlets in the summer and delicious fruits for the birds (and us) later in the year. Quite a lot of moth caterpillars also enjoy the foliage. Ivy is not really good news in a hedge, but left to climb a suitable wall or tree it will flower in the autumn and provide the commas and other autumn butterflies with a good feast of nectar before they go into hibernation. The autumn brood of holly blue caterpillars will also appreciate the flowers and developing fruits, and your garden birds will enjoy the ripe fruits in the spring.

Caterpillars also need food

Nectar-rich flowers will certainly bring a host of butterflies into your garden, but this does not mean that they will stay and breed because the nectar does not usually come from the plants required by the caterpillars. Nevertheless, a good

source of nectar is of great benefit to the visiting species. Your garden is like a service station, where they can re-fuel and maybe rest for a while before moving on. Re-fuelled and refreshed, they are more likely to be successful in finding the food plants on which to lay their eggs, and they will be able to lay more eggs as well.

Unfortunately, the caterpillars of most butterflies feed on weeds, including various grasses, but two food plants well worth having in your garden are sweet rocket and honesty. These will feed both the adults and young of the orange-tip, and if you can find room for a buckthorn bush in your hedge or shrubbery the brimstones are sure to lay some eggs on it.

CONSERVATION TIP

Do not site bird boxes close to your butterfly flowers – certainly not boxes that suit the spotted flycatcher, as this bird will thoroughly enjoy the feast of butterflies.

Identifying butterflies

The butterflies illustrated on these two pages all pass the winter in the adult stage, often sleeping in sheds and gardens. They can be seen stocking up on nectar from michaelmas daisies and other late-flowering plants in the autumn, and they re-appear to feed on aubretia and other spring flowers as early as February. At this time the butterflies often look a bit worse for wear, but this does not prevent them from courting and mating, and laying eggs as soon as their food plants appear.

ABOVE: *The spiky black caterpillars of the peacock butterfly live communally on nettles when young, but disperse as they mature and then pupate on the stems.*

▶ Peacock

Identification: The four eye-spots on the upperside ensure that this butterfly is instantly recognizable. The underside is almost black.
Flight time: June–October and again in spring after hibernation.
Distribution: All but the far north of Europe.
Food plant: Stinging nettle.
Caterpillar: Black and spiky with numerous white dots.
Notes: A strong-flying migrant.

▲ Brimstone

Identification: Male upperside brilliant yellow; female greenish white. Wings never open at rest.
Flight time: June–September and again in spring after hibernation.
Distribution: All but the far north of Europe.
Food plant: Buckthorn and alder buckthorn.
Caterpillar: Blue-green above and lime-green below, with a white stripe on each side.
Notes: Hibernates in shrubs where leaf-like underside gives good camouflage.

▲ Small tortoiseshell

Identification: Look for the blue borders and the extensive black patch at the base of the hindwing. Underside is mottled brown.
Flight time: March–October; usually two broods.
Distribution: All Europe.
Food plant: Stinging nettle.
Caterpillar: Bristly black or dark brown with dense white dots and yellowish sides.
Notes: One of Britain's commonest garden butterflies.

▲ Comma

Identification: The jagged wing margins readily identify this species, named for the comma-shaped white mark under the hindwing.
Flight time: June–September and again in spring after hibernation; two broods.
Distribution: Most of Europe but not Ireland or Scotland.
Food plant: Stinging nettle, elm and hop.
Caterpillar: Black and orange with a white patch at the rear; spiky.
Notes: Summer butterflies often paler than here.

▲ Large tortoiseshell

Identification: This is larger than the small tortoiseshell, with no large black patch on the hindwing. Underside is mottled brown.
Flight time: June–August and again in early spring after hibernation.
Distribution: Most of Europe but a rare visitor to Britain.
Food plant: Elm, sallow and other trees.
Caterpillar: Black with orange streaks and spines. Gregarious.
Notes: Becoming rare everywhere.

▲ Red admiral

Identification: The vivid red patches on the velvety black background are unmistakable.
Flight time: May–October.
Distribution: All Europe.
Food plant: Stinging nettle; adult fond of fruit.
Caterpillar: Usually greyish-black but is sometimes paler; always spiny.
Notes: Once thought to be only a summer visitor to Britain, but now seems to hibernate here in increasing numbers, flying early in spring.

▲ Camberwell beauty

Identification: The cream border makes this species unmistakable.
Flight time: June–August and again in spring after hibernation.
Distribution: Most of Europe but only a rare visitor to Britain.
Food plant: Sallow and other deciduous trees.
Caterpillar: Black and spiky with large orange patches on the back.
Notes: Wing margins are paler after hibernation.

▲ Orange tip

Identification: Only male has orange tips; the female is white. Hindwing mottled green below.
Flight time: April–June.
Distribution: Most of Europe.
Food plant: Honesty, sweet rocket, garlic mustard and various other crucifers – mainly the flowers and seed capsules.
Caterpillar: Bluish-green, speckled with black.
Notes: Rounded wing-tips distinguish female from other whites.

▲ Green-veined white

Identification: Easily recognized by the green lines under the hindwing.
Flight Time: March–November; 2–3 broods.
Distribution: All Europe.
Food plant: Garlic mustard, cuckoo flower, water-cress and various other crucifers; rarely feeds on cultivated brassicas.
Caterpillar: Dull green, speckled with black.
Notes: Summer butterflies have much paler markings than shown here.

ABOVE: *The caterpillar of the black-veined white butterfly is very attractive, but it can be extremely destructive to garden shrubs and fruit trees.*

▲ Black-veined white

Identification: Conspicuous black or brown veins, with no spots.
Flight time: May–July.
Distribution: Most of Europe except the British Isles and the far north.
Food plant: Blackthorn, hawthorn and other rosaceous shrubs, including garden roses.
Caterpillar: Grey and hairy, with black and orange stripes on the back.
Notes: Young caterpillars live in silken tents.

▲ Small white

Identification: White upperside has a small black wing-tip and one (male) or two (female) black spots. Hindwing yellow underneath.
Flight time: March–October; 2–3 broods.
Distribution: All Europe.
Food plant: Numerous wild and cultivated brassicas, and garden nasturtiums.
Caterpillar: Dull green; a yellow stripe on back.
Notes: Summer insects are more heavily marked than spring ones.

▲ Large white

Identification: Creamy white above, with large black wing-tip; female has two spots on upperside of forewing, but male has none.
Flight time: April–October; two broods.
Distribution: All Europe.
Food plant: Mainly cultivated brassicas; also garden nasturtiums.
Caterpillar: Yellow and black, gregarious for much of their lives (see page 15).
Notes: Adults are very fond of buddleia.

▲ Scarce swallowtail

Identification: Six black streaks on each forewing, and long tails on hindwing.
Flight time: March–September: two broods.
Distribution: Southern and central Europe; a rare visitor to the British Isles.
Food plant: Rosaceous trees and shrubs, including garden roses and fruit trees.
Caterpillar: Green and slug-like with red spots and yellow streaks.
Notes: Actually more common than swallowtail.

▲ Swallowtail

Identification: The tails and the black wing-bases readily identify this large butterfly.
Flight time: April–September; 1–3 broods.
Distribution: Most of Europe, but only in Fenland in the British Isles.
Food plant: Various umbellifers, including fennel and wild carrot.
Caterpillar: Plump and green, with black rings and red spots.
Notes: A garden insect only on the continent.

▲ Small skipper

Identification: Bright orange upperside and orange-tipped antennae. Fast, darting flight and, like many skippers, rests with wings separated.
Flight time: May–August.
Distribution: Southern and central Europe; not Scotland or Ireland.
Food plant: Grasses.
Caterpillar: Pale green with yellow stripes; usually concealed in rolled leaf-blade.
Notes: Essex skipper has black tips to antennae.

▲ Painted lady

Identification: The wing colour and pattern, with white spots near the tips, is unmistakable.
Flight time: April–October; two broods.
Distribution: A summer visitor to all Europe.
Food plant: Thistles and, less often, stinging nettle and mallow.
Caterpillar: Black and spiky, dotted with white and lined with yellow.
Notes: Probably unable to survive the winter in Europe; migrates from North Africa each spring.

▲ Wall brown

Identification: The eye-spots readily distinguish this from other orange and brown butterflies. The underside of the hindwing is largely grey.
Flight time: April–October; 2–3 broods.
Distribution: Most of Europe except far north.
Food plant: Coarse grasses.
Caterpillar: Bluish-green with white lines and two short 'tails'.
Notes: The adult butterfly likes to bask on stones and bare ground.

▲ Map butterfly

Identification: This butterfly exists in two very different forms: the spring brood (seen above) and the summer form which is dark brown with a cream or yellow band across each wing.
Flight time: April–September; two broods.
Distribution: Central and southern Europe; absent from the British Isles.
Food plant: Stinging nettle.
Caterpillar: Spiky black with yellowish stripes.
Notes: Named for the map-like underside.

▲ Ringlet

Identification: Readily identified by the band of eye-spots on the underside. Upperside is dark brown, sometimes with faint eye-spots.
Flight time: June–August.
Distribution: Most of Europe except far north.
Food plant: Various grasses.
Caterpillar: Pale brown and bristly, with a darker stripe along the middle and a white stripe on each side; two short 'tails'.
Notes: Adult is very fond of bramble blossom.

▲ Gatekeeper (or hedge brown)

Identification: There are two white pupils in each eye-spot. Female lacks the dark patch in centre of forewing (seen here in the male).
Flight time: July–September.
Distribution: Southern and central Europe; absent from Scotland.
Food plant: Various grasses.
Caterpillar: Pale brown and bristly, with darker spots, white side stripes and two 'tails'.
Notes: Adult is very fond of marjoram flowers.

▲ Holly blue

Identification: Upperside has a slight violet tinge; male has narrower black borders than female seen here. Underside powdery blue with elongate black spots.
Flight time: April–September; two broods.
Distribution: Most of Europe.
Food plant: Holly and various other shrubs in spring; ivy is main food of autumn brood.
Caterpillar: Pale green with a white side stripe.
Notes: The only blue normally in town gardens.

▲ Common blue

Identification: Male is bright violet-blue; female is brown with marginal orange spots. Underside is grey or pale brown with heavy black spots.
Flight time: April–October; 2–3 broods.
Distribution: All Europe.
Food plant: Bird's-foot trefoil, clovers and other legumes.
Caterpillar: Pale green and bristly, with a white side stripe.
Notes: Mainly rural gardens, mostly as a visitor.

▲ Small copper

Identification: Gleaming coppery forewings and barely-marked brown or greyish underside of hindwings distinguish this little butterfly.
Flight time: March-November; 2–3 broods.
Distribution: All Europe.
Food plant: Common and sheep's sorrel; sometimes docks.
Caterpillar: Bright green with pinkish stripes.
Notes: Strongly territorial, an adult butterfly may defend a clump of flowers all day.

Garden moths

Moths are much more numerous than butterflies, with hundreds of species likely to visit your garden during the course of a year. But most of them fly at night.

The best way to see moths in action is to wander round your garden with a torch after dark. A humid, moonless night is best; you will be surprised by how many moths drift silently over the shrubs and flower beds, dropping down to sample the nectar. They usually visit pale, strongly-scented flowers that show up at night.

IDENTIFICATION: BUTTERFLY OR MOTH?

Some colourful moths can be confused with butterflies, but their antennae or feelers will distinguish them. All our butterflies have a little knob at the end of each antenna, whereas most moths' antennae are hair-like or feathery. In addition, almost all moths rest with their wings flat or folded over the body like a tent, with only the uppersides visible. Although many butterflies bask with their wings open, almost all of them rest with their wings closed vertically above the body, so that only the undersides are visible.

ABOVE: *The feathery antennae of many male moths pick up the scent of the females.*

ABOVE: *The clubbed nature of a butterfly's antennae are clearly seen in this skipper.*

ABOVE: *At rest, only the uppersides of the swallowtailed moth's wings are visible.*

ABOVE: *At rest, only the undersides of the orange tip butterfly's wings are visible.*

Concealed or conspicuous?

Most of our moths are decidedly sombre in colour, enabling them to rest undetected on fences and tree trunks or amongst the vegetation by day. Some of their camouflage is truly amazing. They are able to pick out the most suitable backgrounds on which to settle down, and those that resemble bark can even detect the direction of crevices and shuffle themselves around so that their wing patterns are aligned with those of the bark.

Many other moths actually look so similar to twigs or even dead leaves that it takes a really sharp pair of eyes to spot them at rest during the daytime.

However, some garden moths are brightly coloured and very conspicuous indeed. This usually indicates that they are distasteful or even poisonous. Tiger moths and magpie moths are good examples. Once they have tasted them, birds quickly learn to leave these brightly-coloured moths alone.

ABOVE: *Pale thoracic hairs and buff wing tips give the buff-tip moth more than a passing resemblance to a broken twig.*

ABOVE: *The garden tiger moth is extremely conspicuous. This indicates to birds that it is a very distasteful insect.*

HUNGRY CATERPILLARS

Whereas few butterfly caterpillars feed on our garden plants, hundreds of moth caterpillars find our cultivated flowers and vegetables to their liking. In addition to nibbling the leaves, they chew their way through roots and can even be found inside the trunks and branches of trees. Some caterpillars, including those of the mullein and magpie moths, can cause noticeable damage to their food plants, but very few species are sufficiently numerous to spoil the look or the productivity of gardens.

ABOVE: *The larva of the vapourer moth feeds on a wide range of plants and it can damage orchards. Its hairs can cause serious irritation to the skin if it is touched.*

LEFT: *The lilac beauty moth's wings blend in perfectly with a pile of fallen leaves lying in a corner of the garden.*

Identifying moths

Just a few of the common garden moths are illustrated here. When completely at rest, most species conceal their antennae under their wings, but the slightest disturbance brings the antennae forward, as seen in the eyed hawkmoth at the bottom of the page, to detect the source of the problem.

▲ Brimstone moth

Identification: The butter-yellow wings with brown spots are unmistakable.
Flight time: April–October; 1–2 broods.
Distribution: Most of Europe.
Food plant: Hawthorn and many other rosaceous trees and shrubs, including cultivated plums and apples.
Caterpillar: A greyish-brown looper, very twig-like with a twin-pointed hump near the middle.
Notes: Adults readily come to lighted windows.

▲ Lime hawkmoth

Identification: The wings range from green to rusty brown, but always have wavy edges.
Flight time: May–July.
Distribution: Much of Europe except Scotland, Ireland and the far north.
Food plant: Mainly lime, but also elm and alder and some other deciduous trees.
Caterpillar: Pale green with yellow streaks and a horn at the rear.
Notes: Adult lime and eyed hawks do not feed.

▶ Eyed hawkmoth

Identification: Named for the eye-spots on the hindwings. Forewings usually pinkish brown. Always a chocolate patch on the thorax.
Flight time: May–September; two broods.
Distribution: Most of Europe, but not Scotland.
Food plant: Mainly willows and apple.
Caterpillar: Bluish-green with yellow stripes and a terminal horn; usually rests upside-down.
Notes: The moth scares its enemies by suddenly exposing its eye-spots when disturbed.

▲ Elephant hawkmoth

Identification: The green and pink forewings, black and pink hindwings, and white legs readily identify this fast-flying moth.
Flight time: May–July.
Distribution: Most of Europe.
Food plant: Willowherbs, bedstraws and garden fuchsias.
Caterpillar: Dark brown with four eye-spots and a trunk-like snout that gives the insect its name.
Notes: Moth often feeds on honeysuckle at dusk.

▲ Golden plusia

Identification: The golden forewings with a silvery figure-of-eight are unmistakable.
Flight time: June–September.
Distribution: Most of Europe, but rarely seen in Ireland.
Food plant: Mainly delphiniums in the garden.
Caterpillar: Leaf green with white spots and lines; only three pairs of stumpy prolegs.
Notes: Caterpillar gnaws through leaf veins, causing leaf to collapse around it like a tent.

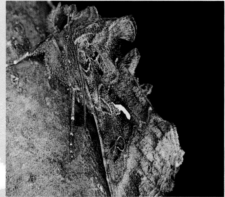

▲ Barred yellow

Identification: The colour and pattern readily identify this little moth.
Flight time: May–July.
Distribution: Most of Europe except for the far northern areas.
Food plant: Wild and cultivated roses.
Caterpillar: A pale green looper with yellow bands and a dark stripe along the back.
Notes: This hedgerow moth commonly rests with its abdomen pointing upwards.

▲ Silver Y

Identification: Named for the silver 'Y' in the middle of the velvety-grey to black forewings.
Flight time: May–November.
Distribution: All Europe, but only as a summer visitor in Britain and all northern regions.
Food plant: A wide range of herbaceous plants.
Caterpillar: Plump and green with only three pairs of fleshy legs at the rear.
Notes: Flies by night and day, usually seen as a grey blur hovering at flowers.

Attracting moths

If you have ever left the curtains open in a lighted room on a summer night, you will know that moths are attracted to lights: the window panes can be covered with the insects. This simple method can tell you a good deal about the moths in your garden, but a stronger light and a white sheet will reveal even more. Hang the sheet from a washing line, or simply spread it on the lawn, and shine the light on it. On a warm, overcast night the moths will stream in and they will often settle down on the sheet so that you can examine and identify them.

Sweet tongues

Many moths can be attracted to a sugary mixture daubed on walls or tree trunks. Every moth enthusiast has his or her own recipe, but rum, beer and molasses usually feature prominently. Mixed to a fairly thick consistency so that it does not run, it should be applied in narrow vertical patches at about head-height – high enough not to spoil your clothes if you accidentally lean on the surface. The moths sit around the edges of the meal and push their tongues into it until they have had their fill. Again, you need to sit up late to see them.

Moths attracted by light or sugar will not necessarily be living in your garden, but mated females may stay around long enough to lay eggs on the plants. Most of

RIGHT: *A convolvulus hawkmoth probes some beauty-of-the-night flowers with a tongue which is about as long as its body.*

your visitors will actually be males, as these are the ones flying around in search of mates and most likely to be attracted, or perhaps distracted, by your light or sugar patches. The females are usually busy laying their eggs.

Flowers for moths

Pale-coloured flowers that open and release their scent at night provide the best re-fuelling stations for moths, so a moth garden should include night-scented stock,

nicotiana (tobacco flower) and honeysuckle. Sweet Williams also attract plenty of moths, but one of the best for attracting the long-tongued hawkmoths is the beauty-of-the-night, which is also known as the marvel of Peru. Its slender, tubular flowers, ranging from white through yellow to red, open their nectar stores in late afternoon. Pussy willow catkins also sustain many moths in the spring.

LEFT: *The herald moth hibernates in the adult state and can often be found in sheds and cellars in the winter. It usually adopts a head-down position and is easily mistaken for a dead leaf.*

WILDLIFE PROJECT – TRAPPING MOTHS

If you use just a sheet and a lamp, you need to stay up late yourself to see the moths, so you might prefer to use some form of trap around the light. Portable traps, powered by mains electricity or car batteries, can be bought from biological supply companies, but it is not difficult to make a simple trap with a large cardboard box.

◆ Cut a hole in the top of the box to take a large plastic funnel, and put several sheets of egg-packing inside.

◆ Suspend an ordinary lamp of 150–200 watts directly above the funnel to attract plenty of moths.

◆ Moths hitting the light fall through the funnel and into the box, where they settle down comfortably in the hollows of the egg-packing. They can be examined in the morning and released unharmed.

◆ The trap can be left on all night, but the lamp must have a transparent shield over it to protect it from rain. Cold rain hitting the hot lamp may cause it to shatter.

SAFETY TIP When using mains electricity, always ensure that all electrical connections are suitable for outdoor use and are well protected from rain and dew.

ABOVE: *The following morning, you can carefully remove the egg-packing from the moth trap to study the captured moths before releasing them back into the wild. Trapped moths are quite sleepy in the morning and easily examined.*

BELOW: *Commercially available traps like this use ultra-violet lamps. They attract more moths than ordinary light bulbs.*

Bees and wasps

Bees and wasps all belong to the large order of insects that is known as the Hymenoptera. There is, however, one big difference in the behaviour of the two groups: bees all feed their youngsters with pollen and nectar, whereas wasps rear their grubs on a diet of meat, usually insects or spiders.

Asked to name some bees, most people are likely to come up with just two: the honey bee and the bumble bee. Gardeners may add the leaf-cutter bee, but there are actually over 250 different kinds of bees in the British Isles. The adults feed primarily on nectar and, although by no means all of them are likely to occur in your garden, they all play a major role in pollinating our wild and cultivated flowers, including fruit crops (see below).

Dancing bees

On each expedition from its hive, a honey bee tends to visit just one kind of flower, so pollen is not wasted on flowers where it cannot effect pollination. This makes honey bees particularly good pollinators. Fruit growers often borrow beehives when their trees are in flower to guarantee successful pollination of the blossom and a good fruit crop – and the bee keepers benefit from a good yield of honey, which the bees make from the nectar.

The bees are incredibly efficient at collecting nectar because an individual finding a good source tells the rest of the colony about it by 'dancing' when it returns to the hive. The direction and speed of the dance tells other workers exactly where to find the nectar, and they fly out to gather it.

You can get a reasonably good idea of the efficiency of this recruitment by putting a spoonful of honey or strong sugar solution on a saucer and persuading a bee to drink from it. This is not as difficult as you might think: if you dip a small twig in some honey and hold it close to a bee on a flower, the bee will readily transfer its attention to the honey and you can carry it to the saucer. Mark the bee with a small spot of non-toxic paint while it is feeding and then watch it fly off. As long as its hive is not too far away, you may well find it back with a gang of friends in a few minutes.

RIGHT: *The small flowers of* Photinia davidii *(see page 119) literally ooze with nectar, which is being sampled here by a honey bee. There are several races of honey bees, each differing slightly in colour but all usually with conspicuous pale bands on their abdomen.*

Hairy bumbles

Bumble bees are generally bigger and furrier than honey bees. There are 25 British species, although some are very rare and only half a dozen are likely to occur in the garden. They usually nest in the ground, often in hedge-banks, and their colonies rarely contain more than a few hundred individuals, whereas a honey bee colony may contain over 50,000 insects. Bumble bees also differ from honey bees in that their colonies last for just a few months. Only the mated females (queens) survive the winter and they start new colonies in the spring. Bumble bees make no combs and do not store much honey, but they are still important pollinators.

Many bumble bee species have become noticeably rarer in recent years.

FLOWERS FOR BEES

Try growing some of the following flowers to encourage bees into your garden:
- Borage
- Foxglove
- Globe thistle
- Helichrysum (everlasting straw flower)
- Knapweed
- Lungwort
- Marjoram
- Poppies (especially the opium poppy)
- Red clover
- Red deadnettle (various cultivars)
- Sage
- Teasel

The loss of our flower-rich meadows and roadside verges may have contributed to the decline, together with the loss of many miles of hedgerow nesting

LEFT: *Copious supplies of both nectar and pollen mean that the little hover-fly on the right can feed happily alongside the much larger bumble bee on this colourful helichrysum flower.*

habitats. You can help to restore the fortunes of the bees by planting nectar-rich flowers and providing artificial homes (see page 119).

BELOW: *Guided by the dark spots, a bumble bee makes its way right inside a foxglove flower to sample the rich supply of nectar at the top of the bell. While feeding, the bee will be liberally dusted with pollen, much of which will be carried home in the pollen baskets on its back legs.*

LEFT: *The wool carder bee nests in holes in wood. She gathers and combs plant hairs with her toothed jaws and mixes them with saliva to line her nest and make the cells for her eggs.*

Living alone

The majority of bees are solitary insects, with each female working alone to make a small nest. Each nest consists of a few cells and may be excavated in the ground, in dead wood or in hollow stems and other crevices. Leaf-cutter bees are well known to gardeners because they make their nests with sections of leaves cut from roses and other plants.

Other solitary bees make their nest cells with sand or mud, with fibres plucked from plants, or with the sawdust created while excavating in wood. The cells are stocked with a mixture of pollen and nectar and an egg is laid in each one. The female then seals the cells and flies away. She has no contact with her offspring. It is easy to encourage these useful and interesting insects to settle in your garden by providing them with suitable nest sites (see pages 118–119).

SAFETY TIP

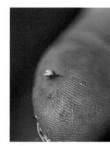

Solitary bees and wasps rarely sting us, and even the social ones are not usually very aggressive as long as you don't stand in front of their nests. Their stings can be painful, but the pain is usually short-lived. If you are stung by a honey bee the strongly-barbed sting will stay in your skin. Don't try to pull it out with tweezers, as this will just force more poison into you. Scraping it out is a much better way to deal with it.

WHAT GOOD IS A WASP?

Few people have a good word to say for wasps, and many immediately reach for the insecticide or a rolled-up newspaper when one appears, which is a pity because they really do a lot of good in the garden!

The most familiar of the 180 or so British wasps are the social species, several of which nest in and around our homes and often cause consternation or even panic around the tea table in the autumn. These black and yellow insects build ball-shaped nests with paper, which they make themselves from wood pulp. In spring and summer you can often see, and even hear, wasps scraping wood from sheds and fence posts. Mixed with saliva, the wood is moulded into tiny strips, thousands of which are joined together to form the nest. A completed nest consists of several tiers of hexagonal cells enclosed by a number of insulating sheets. Some species hang their nests in trees and shrubs, while others build in hedge banks or in roof spaces and other cavities in buildings.

Thousands of grubs are reared in the cells and the inhabitants of a single nest munch through something like 250,000 insects during the summer. Many of these are harmful caterpillars and flies – a point worth remembering when you are tempted to reach for the aerosol. Like the bumble bee

ABOVE: *This queen wasp is using her strong jaws to gather wood fragments, which she will turn into strips of paper.*

colonies, our wasp colonies are annual affairs, with only mated females surviving the winter.

Less than half of our British wasps sport the black and yellow coloration that most people associate with wasps. Many are jet black. The great majority are solitary creatures, nesting in burrows and crevices in much the same way as the solitary bees but stocking their nests with paralyzed insects or spiders. Some specialize in aphids or small caterpillars, and are therefore friends of the gardener, whereas others stick to various flies.

Solitary wasps can be encouraged into the garden in the same way as the solitary bees. Few people will want to encourage the social wasps to nest in their garden, but as long as they do not settle too close to the house or other regularly-used areas there is no need to destroy them.

LEFT: *Wasp colonies break up in the autumn when they have finished rearing their young and, with no more work to do, the insects turn their full attention to our fruit and other sweet things – a just reward perhaps for their earlier pest-controlling activities.*

ABOVE: *Many harmless insects, including hover-flies (top) and clearwing moths (above), mimic wasps to good effect. Birds and other predators that have learned that wasps are unpleasant leave the similarly-coloured mimics alone as well.*

The bee hotel

The solitary bees are excellent pollinators of our garden plants – especially in the spring, when they can be seen foraging on fruit trees and bushes. The tawny mining bee is one of many species that nest in the ground, and its little volcano-shaped mounds can often be seen on the lawn in the spring. Others tunnel into wood and even into soft mortar, so don't be in too much of a hurry to re-point old garden walls; the bees will not do much harm as long as not too many of them choose the same patch of wall.

Although most bees are prepared to do some digging when preparing their nests, they are generally happy to accept ready-made tunnels. The harebell carpenter bee, which feeds almost exclusively on pollen and nectar from campanulas, is small enough to be able to use old woodworm holes in sheds and fences.

You can attract this and many other solitary bees by constructing a 'bee hotel'. This consists of one or more planks of wood, 10–15 cm (4–6 in) thick, drilled with numerous holes ranging from 2–10 mm ($1/12$–$2/5$ in) in diameter. Fix the planks to a wall or a fence in a sheltered, south-facing position and then watch the bees select their 'rooms' and stock them ready for egg-laying. A large log or a tree stump drilled with holes is equally acceptable to the bees. With about a quarter of Britain's native bees now listed as endangered species, anything that you can do to help them must be a good thing.

Solitary wasps will also use the 'hotel', and watching them will reveal that each species stocks its nest with a particular kind of prey – mostly aphids, caterpillars or flies, although some wasps prefer to hunt spiders.

WILDLIFE PROJECT – A FLOWER POT NEST

A flower pot with a diameter of about 15 cm (6 in) makes an acceptable bumble bee home. Part-fill it with old mouse bedding and bury it on its side in a bank of soil. Ensure that the drain hole is visible and a queen bumble bee might well take up residence. Alternatively, invert the flower pot on a small paving slab, overlapping the edge so that there is a small gap for the bees to get in. Plug the drain hole to keep the rain out.

LEFT: *Hollow canes or other tubes up to a centimetre in diameter make great homes for solitary bees. Pack them into a tin or a length of drain pipe 15 cm (6 in) long. Make sure that the bees can enter only at one end; if you use a length of drain pipe, you will have to block up the ends of the tubes with modelling wax.*

Bumble bee homes

Bumble bees usually nest on or under the ground, often in old mouse nests in well-drained banks. They sometimes accept artificial homes, and a simple wooden box with a couple of 15 mm (2/3 in) holes in the sides makes a good bumble bee home. Stuff it with old mouse or gerbil bedding – scrounged from the pet shop if you have no pets of your own – and bury it in a pile of leaf litter at the base of a hedge so that the holes are just visible. Do this in early spring, when the queens are searching for nest sites. If it is accepted, you will be able to watch the coming and going of the bees throughout the summer. A medium-sized flower pot, buried in a bank with the drain hole just visible, may also be acceptable to bees.

Flowers for bumble bees

Although bumble bees are particularly attracted to deep-throated blue and purple flowers, such as foxgloves and sage, they feed at a wide range of flowers. Lungwort is a good source of food early in the spring, but for attracting and feeding the insects later in the spring you can't beat *Photinia davidii*, also known as *Stranvaesia davidii* (see page 115). The small creamy flowers of this evergreen shrub attract so many worker bees with their slightly sickly scent in May that a bush in full flower can be 'heard' from several metres away. Your garden birds will also enjoy the red berries later in the year.

FAR LEFT: Dozens of solitary bees, of several different species, may take up residence in a simple 'bee hotel', made from a thick plank screwed to the wall.

119

Dragonflies

Despite their fast and often noisy flight, and country names such as 'horse stingers' and 'devil's darning needles', these beautiful, gauzy-winged creatures are quite harmless and should be welcome in any garden. They catch huge numbers of mosquitoes and other troublesome flies and, being among our largest insects, they are easy to watch.

Dragons and damsels

The larger species, which always rest with their wings outstretched, are often called true dragonflies. Their great eyes, each with up to 30,000 tiny lenses, can spot the slightest movement, and their amazing manoeuvrability enables the insects to change direction instantly to grab their

RIGHT: *Breeding in many garden ponds, the large red damselfly is often on the wing in April and is one of the first species to appear in the spring.*

prey in mid air. Victims are scooped up by the spiky legs, which are held under the head like a net. Hawker dragonflies each adopt a territory, such as a hedgerow, and patrol it for hours on end, snatching any prey that comes within range and also seeing off other dragonflies, often with a clashing of wings at the edge of the territory. Darter dragonflies spend most of their time on a perch, from which they dart out to catch passing prey.

The smaller dragonflies, which usually rest with their wings vertically above their slender bodies, are called damselflies. Slower and more delicate altogether, they prefer to pluck aphids and other small insects from the vegetation.

Watery beginnings

Dragonflies all grow up in water and, although the larger species may well visit gardens far from water, you are most likely to attract them if you have your own pond. The more sedentary damselflies are unlikely to be seen in your garden unless you or one of your

LEFT: *Azure damselflies display the group's unique mating posture: the male holds the female's neck while she curves her body forward to contact the front of his abdomen.*

LEFT: The life cycle of the dragonfly begins when the female lays her eggs in the water.

close neighbours has a pond. A good pond will encourage both groups to breed. Ideally, you need some emergent plants that the young insects can climb when about to change into adults and also some floating plants on which the adults can bask. Many species also need vegetation to support them while laying their eggs, and don't forget one or two prominent perches for the darters – canes pushed into the surrounding ground are fine, especially if they overhang the water.

If you see a dragonfly bobbing over the pond surface and periodically dipping its abdomen into the water, it will be a female laying eggs. Some species cling to the vegetation and push their abdomen into the water to lay eggs on or in the submerged stems, and in a number of species the male actually holds the female by the neck while she deposits her eggs. The pair even fly in this tandem position while looking for suitable sites.

You are most likely to see the young stages – the nymphs – when pulling out

excess vegetation or removing mud from the bottom of the pond in the autumn. Generally dark grey with long legs, they are equipped with a fearsome lower jaw that can be shot out to impale other small creatures. It is called the mask because it covers the mouth when not in use.

LEFT: A nymph may spend several years in the water before climbing a plant stem and splitting its skin to release the new adult.

Ladybirds

Every gardener can easily recognize a ladybird, and there can be very few people who do not know that these colourful beetles are our valuable allies in the constant struggle against aphids and several other insect pests.

ABOVE: *The ladybird larva looks nothing like the adult, but it is equally effective at controlling aphids in the garden.*

RIGHT: *Aphids may kick and struggle, but they are no match for the ladybird's tough jaws.*

BELOW: *Large numbers of ladybirds may hibernate in secluded corners, emerging to sun themselves en masse in the spring.*

There is not a lot that you can do to encourage ladybirds into your garden, but if your roses or other plants are suffering from a severe plague of aphids you can try collecting some ladybirds from the wild. Put them on the infested plants and they will probably stay there until they have polished off the aphids, although not all aphids are eaten with equal enthusiasm. The big aphids that wreck lupin flowers, for example, are avoided by most ladybirds.

You can also buy ladybird cultures from various suppliers, but don't be surprised when you receive a collection of bluish-grey grubs instead of the familiar beetles. These are the ladybird larvae. They are common enough in the garden, but many gardeners do not know what they are and all too many are squashed in the belief that they are nibbling the plants, but the larvae are just as good at eating aphids as their parents and each one can eat over 100 aphids in a week. That's perhaps as many as 500 before it reaches its full size and turns into an adult to continue the carnage.

Colourful warnings

The ladybirds' bright colours warn birds and other predators that the insects taste foul. You will be aware of their flavour if you handle them. They literally bleed on your hands and leave long-lasting, pungent stains. Birds have only to try one or two ladybirds before they learn to leave them alone.

Vegetarian ladybirds

Although most of the ladybirds are entirely predatory, there are some vegetarian species, including the 22-spot ladybird. Named for the 22 little black dots on its yellow wing cases, this tiny creature eats mildews and is often to be found on gooseberry and currant bushes in the spring.

Spiders

A small garden may well contain several thousand spiders. There will be many secretive, ground-living hunters as well as the more familiar web-spinning species whose webs are so conspicuous when studded with dew or frost in the autumn.

The webs are extremely effective traps for a variety of flying and crawling insects and, although they clearly claim many harmless and useful creatures, they do undoubtedly account for a lot of pests. The spiders are therefore important components of the garden fauna, and they are also fascinating creatures to watch although, with the dislike of these animals being almost universal, few people are prepared to get close to them.

Spiders can make a living almost anywhere and there is no need to do anything to encourage them into the garden other than to provide a diversity of habitats. And the more habitats you create, the more spider species you are likely to have. They will take up residence in the hedge, on the fence and the garden

LEFT: *The garden spider spins its more or less circular web on shrubs and fences. It usually spins a new web each day because insects and wind often break the silk and reduce the web to an ineffective tangle of threads, as seen here.*

wall, in the log-pile, on the rockery and around your doors and windows. The cute little zebra spider is even happy on bare house walls. With the exception of a few Mediterranean species that can pack a painful bite, none of our European spiders is harmful to the gardener, so do take a closer look at your eight-legged guests.

ABOVE: *The nursery web spider, seen carrying its egg sac, hunts on plants. It spins a tent-like web to protect its offspring – hence its name.*

LEFT: *The zebra spider is one of the jumping spiders and is very common on walls and fences where it picks out its insect prey with its huge front eyes and then jumps on to it from a distance of several centimetres.*

Keeping a record

Having created your wildlife garden, and undoubtedly attracted a wide range of fascinating animal visitors, you will hopefully want to keep a record of their comings and goings throughout the year.

Memory is notoriously unreliable and a diary or notebook is indispensable for keeping an accurate record. Start it as soon as you embark on wildlife gardening and write down what you see each day. If you are starting a garden or any particular feature, such as a pond, from scratch it is worth recording the stages at which the various plants and animals first put in an appearance. In this way, you will be able to appreciate how the community evolves as the garden matures. Record what the animals are doing as well as simply the dates on which you see them.

It is particularly valuable to note the kind of food that each species prefers, as this will help you to work out the best foods to offer on your bird table and elsewhere in your garden. Record the dates on which you first notice the birds singing and courting, when they start to collect nesting materials, and when they start to take food back to the nest, indicating that one or other of the pair is sitting on eggs or that the eggs have already hatched. If you can link your observations to the weather you might be able to work out what causes animals or flowers to appear earlier or later in any particular year.

CHOOSING BINOCULARS

Looking at a pair of ordinary binoculars, you should see two figures somewhere. The first figure indicates the magnifying power of the binoculars, and the second is the diameter of the objective lens – the lens furthest from your eye. For example, a 9 x 40 pair has a magnification of x 9 and objective lenses 40 mm in diameter. This is probably the best size for general use, and certainly ideal for use in the garden. Another good size is 8 x 30, but binoculars with objectives less than 30 mm in diameter are less effective for following birds in flight. They are also less satisfactory in dull weather because they do not gather in enough light. More powerful ones do not generally focus closer than about 10 m (30 ft) and are less suitable for garden use. Zoom binoculars, providing variable degrees of magnification in a single instrument, can be very useful, although they are more expensive. Some will give you a magnification of x 100, but you are unlikely to want such power in the garden. Look for a pair marked 10–30 x 30, which will give magnifications from x 10 to x 30 with objective lenses 30 mm in diameter. Always test binoculars thoroughly before buying, making sure that they are comfortable to use and that there is no distortion of the image. Having chosen the size and type you want, always buy the best pair you can afford.

A closer look

A well-sited bird table will enable you to watch your feathered visitors with the naked eye, but a pair of binoculars can make things even more exciting. They are essential for watching some of the shyer garden birds, and will also enable you to get a good look at dragonflies and butterflies that don't like you to get too close. At the other end of the spectrum, you will need a magnifying glass to watch caterpillars chomping their way through leaves and bees collecting pollen. An old-fashioned reading glass with a short handle can be very useful, but for appreciating the exquisite beauty of insect eggs and other tiny objects you will need a lens with a magnification of at least x 10. Whatever you choose, keep it on a string around your neck, otherwise you are sure to drop it into the long grass or, even more annoyingly, your pond.

Film and video

Most people interested in wildlife like to take photographs or make videos of the plants and animals around them, and this is a great way to create a permanent record of your garden. A bewildering array of modern cameras is available to you. Digital cameras can create fantastic pictures for you to watch on your television, but cameras for transparencies and colour prints are still very popular.

I use a single-lens reflex camera, which for much of the time is fitted with a 90 mm macro lens. Although this is rather heavy, it does allow me to get good close-ups of insects as well as more

distant views without changing lenses. Whatever camera you eventually choose, you do need to be able to over-ride the automatic exposure settings, otherwise pale subjects on dark backgrounds will be washed out and vice-versa. You will also need electronic flash for most close-ups and subjects in shady spots.

If you plan to video your garden, try to tell a story – from the early stages through to maturity, for example, or perhaps an account of a year in the garden. Avoid filming everything at the same time of day, and when editing the tapes try not to jump rapidly from one thing to another. Short sequences of activity, such as a hedge turning green in spring, are far more stimulating than a series of 'snap-shots', and if you produce nothing more than a catalogue of your garden wildlife you might as well concentrate on still photography instead.

Spread the word

Show your photographs or films to local garden clubs and wildlife groups. Your enthusiasm can be infectious and this is one of the best ways to encourage others to take up wildlife gardening.

Useful information

Suppliers of bird foods, bird tables and nest boxes

CJ WildBird Foods Ltd
The Rea, Upton Magna,
Shrewsbury SY4 4UR
www.birdfood.co.uk
Foods, feeding devices, artificial homes and much more for all your garden wildlife.

J.E. Haith Ltd
65 Park Street, Cleethorpes,
N.E. Lincolnshire
DN35 7NF
www.haiths.com
Everything for the birds and the bird-watcher.

The Royal Society for the Protection of Birds
The Lodge, Sandy,
Bedfordshire SG19 2DL
www.rspb.org.uk
Working for a healthy environment rich in birds and wildlife.

Suppliers of wild flower seeds and plants, including native trees and shrubs

Buckingham Nurseries and Garden Centre
Tingewick Road, Buckingham
MK18 4AE

Fothergill's Seeds
Gazely Road, Kentford,
Newmarket, Suffolk CB8 7QB

John Chambers
15 Westleigh Road, Barton
Seagrave, Kettering,
Northants NN15 5AJ

NPK Landscapes
Grove Hill, Old Edinburgh Road,
Newton Stewart DG8 6PL
www.npk.u-net.com

National Wildflower Centre
Court Hey Park, Liverpool
L16 3NA
www.wildflower.org.uk

Naturescape
Maple Farm, Coach Gap Lane,
Langer, Nottinghamshire
NG13 9HP
www.naturescape.co.uk

Y.S.J. Seeds
Kingsfield Conservation
Nursery, Broadenham Lane,
Winsham, Chard, Somerset
TA20 4JF

Yellow Flag Wildflowers
8 Plock Court, Longford,
Gloucestershire GL2 9DW
www.wildflowersuk.com

Other organizations

The Bat Conservation Trust
15 Cloisters House, 8 Battersea
Park Road, London SW8 4BG
www.bats.org.uk
Advice on bats and their conservation.

Butterfly Conservation
Manor Yard, East Lulworth,
Wareham,
Dorset BH20 5QP
www.butterfly-conservation.org
Advice and information on all aspects of butterfly conservation and gardening.

Froglife
Mansion House, 27–28
Market Place, Halesworth,
Suffolk IP19 8AY
www.froglife.org
Working to conserve the native amphibians and reptiles of Britain and Ireland.

The Green Gardener
47 Strumpshaw Road, Brundall,
Norfolk NR13 5PG
Suppliers of lacewings, ladybirds and other biological control agents, plus wildlife homes and other 'green' commodities.

Henry Doubleday Research Association
Ryton Organic Gardens,
Ryton-on-Dunsmore,
Coventry CV8 3LG
www.hdra.org.uk
Information on all aspects of organic gardening.

London Wildlife Trust Centre for Wildlife Gardening
28 Marsden Road, London
SE15 4EE
www.wildlondon.org.uk

Useful websites

www.nhm.ac.uk/science/projects/fff
This website enables you to find out which wild plants are native to your area simply by entering the first part of your postcode.

www.greenfingers.com
A website offering wildlife gardening tips.

www.which.net/gardeningwhich/advice/ wildflowers.html
Gardening Which? website which has fact sheets listing native tree, shrub and seed suppliers. Advice sheets on Wildflowers for the Garden *and* Making a Mini Meadow *are also available from their website.*

Bibliography

Birdfeeder Handbook, Robert Burton (Dorling Kindersley 1991)

Creating a Flower Meadow, Yvette Verner (Green Books 1998)

Creating a Wildlife Garden, Bob & Liz Gibbons (Chancellor 1996)

Dry Stone Walling: A Practical Handbook, Alan Brooks and Sean Adcock (British Trust for Conservation Volunteers)

Feed the Birds, Tony Soper (David & Charles 1991)

Garden Creepy Crawlies, Michael Chinery (Whittet 1986)

Garden Plants for Butterflies, Matthew Oates (Brian Masterton & Associates 1985)

Garden Wildlife of Britain and Europe, Michael Chinery (HarperCollins 1997) A photographic guide to the wild plants and animals that can be found in the garden.

Gardening for Butterflies, Margaret Vickery (Butterfly Conservation 1988) Contains a wealth of information on attracting and identifying butterflies in Britain.

How to Attract Butterflies to Your Garden, John & Maureen Tampion (Guild of Master Craftsmen Publications 2003) All you need to know about attracting butterflies in Europe.

How to Make a Wildlife Garden, Chris Baines (Elm Tree 1985)

The Natural Stone Directory (QMJ Publishing)

The Natural History of the Garden, Michael Chinery (Collins 1977)

The New Bird Table Book, Tony Soper (David & Charles 1973)

Urban Wildlife, Peter Shirley (Whittet Books 1996)

Wildlife Begins at Home, Tony Soper (David & Charles 1975)

The publishers would like to thank CJ Wildbird Foods for their kind assistance in providing many of the photographs of their bird and animal products. For further information go to: www.birdfood.co.uk

Index